FINDING YOUR WAY TO
Wellness
PUGET SOUND BREAST CANCER
INFORMATION & RESOURCE GUIDE

℘

Susan G. Komen for the Cure

Puget Sound Affiliate

[THIRD EDITION]

Published by Susan G. Komen for the Cure, Puget Sound Affiliate
1900 Northlake Way, Suite 237
Seattle, WA 98103
206/633-0303
www.komenseattle.org

ISBN 0-9674187-1-2

Book design: Kate Basart/Union Pageworks
Copy editor: Julie Van Pelt
Produced by Unleashed Book Development
Cover artwork: *Spirit Healer,* by Joan Bowman
Printed in the United States

Catalog records for this book are available from the Library of Congress.

This book is dedicated to all the women who feel alone as they

face the biggest challenge of their lives: breast cancer.

Many have walked before you—and found their way to wellness.

Many walk beside you—and offer their hands and hearts.

Take their hands, open your heart. And you will not walk alone.

—Kate Rose Kilpatrick

Authors of the third edition:

Julie Gralow
Heather Bybee
Jean Christ
Pat Dawson
Leah DeRoulet
Joan Elvin
Polly Halpern
Dan Labriola
Barbara Lees
Constance Lehman
Andrea Leiserowitz
Angela Lim
Hannah Linden
Stephanie Martin
Janet Parker
Barbara Silko
Jean Stern
Pam Tazioli
Susan Yaszay

ॐ

Acknowledgments:

Wendy Berry
Ann McMurray
Prioska Maggasy
Amy Myers
Sue Way
Kenneth Willer
Susan G. Komen for the Cure
Volunteers

This newest edition of *Finding Your Way to Wellness* could not have been written without the dedicated research and assistance of previous contributors. We honor their lives and their legacies in the ongoing effort to eradicate breast cancer as a life threatening disease.

FIRST EDITION:

Julie Gralow
Alice Burgess
Pat Clemence
Julia Canas
Mary Berg
Cathleen Carr
Becky Galentine
Susan Goedde
Kathy Kirk
Julie Kirschbaum
Pat Chikamoto Lee
Alyson Longley
Cathy Ruiz
Linda Tatta
Clo Wilson-Hashiguchi

SECOND EDITION:

Julie Gralow
Denise Bowls
Alice Burgess
Julia Canas
Kim Dammann
Pat Dawson
Debra Forman
Susan Goedde
Dan Labriola
Elizabeth Landrum
Barbara Lees
Alison Longley
Stephanie Martin
Patti McConnell
Janet Parker
Marisa Perdomo
Martha Purrier
Kate Rose Kilpatrick
Sandra Saffle
C. J. Taylor
Elizabeth J. White

Contents

As I walk

My shadow stretched out before me

I am in the eternal present

I am here and now

Focused on being

—Carolyn Plant, Breast Cancer Survivor

❧

The First Step Is Information

Facing a diagnosis of breast cancer can be overwhelming for patients, their family members and their friends. All newly diagnosed patients can benefit from up-to-date information on breast cancer, including how it is diagnosed, what treatment options are available, how to manage treatment side effects and where to find helpful resources. Recognizing this need, the Puget Sound Affiliate of Susan G. Komen for the Cure has produced *Finding Your Way to Wellness: Puget Sound Breast Cancer Information and Resource Guide.*

This is the third edition of *Finding Your Way to Wellness.* Thousands of copies of the first two editions have been provided to breast cancer patients in the Puget Sound region since 1996. The guide was created in an effort to make information gathering easier and quicker. This new edition includes an overview of breast cancer, with references for obtaining further information as well as listings of local and national resources available to breast cancer patients. The guide was written by a volunteer group of breast cancer survivors and health care professionals in the Puget Sound area. Susan G. Komen for the Cure does not endorse specific organizations or resources listed in this guide.

It is our hope that this guide will help you through the challenging journey that follows a diagnosis of breast cancer. In order to stay updated on new information, programs, treatments and research options within the field of breast cancer, we encourage readers to communicate with their health care team and to contact Susan G. Komen for the Cure and other breast cancer organizations listed in this guide.

We welcome your feedback as well as suggestions for resources and information to be included in future editions of this book. Should you have updates, comments or corrections, please contact the Puget Sound Affiliate of Susan G. Komen for the Cure at 206/633-0303. Additional copies of this guide may also be obtained by calling this number.

I was diagnosed with infiltrating ductal carcinoma, an 8-cm tumor in my left breast with lymph node involvement in October. It was the last thing that I expected to be told. My treatment consisted of chemo every week for six months. I then had a bi-lateral mastectomy followed by seven weeks of radiation. Cancer was not a welcome intrusion in my life. As with most experiences in life, however, something lost is something gained. I lost my breasts, but gained more than I could ever have imagined personally.

—*Julie Kofoed, diagnosed in 2002 at age 39*

꠹

Chapter 1

The Breast Cancer "Epidemic"

B reast cancer is the most frequently diagnosed cancer among U.S. women, other than skin cancer. Approximately 1 in 8 women in the United States who live to be 90 will be diagnosed with breast cancer. An average woman's chance of getting breast cancer is about 1 in 200 by age 40, 1 in 24 between ages 40 and 59, and 1 in 13 between ages 60 and 79. Approximately 80 percent of women diagnosed with breast cancer in the United States are over the age of 50, and half of all cases occur in women 65 years and older. Although less common, breast cancer in younger women also occurs.

The American Cancer Society estimates that, in 2006, 212,920 women and 1,720 men will be diagnosed with invasive breast cancer in the United States. In Washington State in 2006, 4,000 women are predicted to be diagnosed with *invasive* breast cancer. In addition, 61,980 new cases of noninvasive *(in situ)* breast cancer are expected to occur in U.S. women in 2006. Of these occurrences, approximately 85 percent will be ductal carcinoma in situ (DCIS). The increase in DCIS cases is a direct result of increased use of screening mammography, which can detect breast cancers before they are felt.

In the 1980s, breast cancer incidence rates increased by as much as 4 percent per year. This has sometimes been called a breast cancer "epidemic." Increased use of screening mammography certainly contributed to this increase in breast cancer incidence, resulting in earlier and more frequent detection of cancer. Additionally, national trends related to lifestyle and reproductive factors, including nutrition, physical activity, obesity or being overweight, number of pregnancies and age at first pregnancy and the common use of postmenopausal hormone replacement therapy, also undoubtedly played a role. Breast cancer incidence rates have leveled off in the United States in recent years.

Although 1 in 8 women in the United States will develop breast cancer, only 1 in 33 will die from this disease. The American Cancer Society estimates that 40,970 women and 460 men will die from breast cancer in 2006. Breast cancer ranks second among cancer deaths in U.S. women (after lung cancer). According to recent data, breast cancer death rates decreased by 2.3 percent per year from 1990 to 2001 in all women, with larger decreases in young women (aged 50 years or less). This is likely due to the combination of increased awareness, earlier detection and better treatment.

The five-year survival rate for patients with *localized* breast cancer has increased from 80 percent in the 1950s to 98 percent today. If the cancer has spread regionally (beyond the breast to the lymph nodes), the five-year survival rate is 80 percent. For women diagnosed with distant metastases, 26 percent will be alive at five years. Of all women diagnosed with breast cancer of any stage, 77 percent will survive ten years. There are presently over 2 million breast cancer survivors alive in the United States.

For more information on breast cancer incidence and survival rates, visit the American Cancer Society's website at www.cancer.org. Information in this chapter is from *Breast Cancer Facts and Figures 2005-2006*, available at that website.

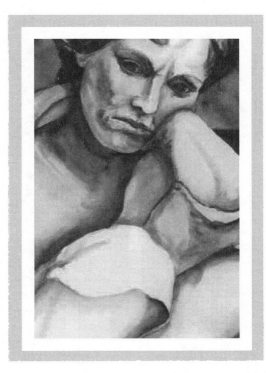

Decisions

—*Lori Vermillion, Breast Cancer Survivor*

❧

Chapter 2

Breast Cancer Risk Factors, Genetics and Risk Reduction (Prevention)

The development and progression of breast cancer are the result of several *mutations* or alterations in the DNA of normal breast tissue. It is still not clear what causes the DNA changes that lead to breast cancer, or how to prevent them from occurring. The development of breast cancer appears to result from a combination of many factors. Researchers are investigating the roles of genetics, lifestyle, environment and *hormones*.

Breast Cancer Risk Factors and Genetics

GENDER AND AGE: The two most significant risk factors for developing breast cancer are being a woman and getting older. Ninety-five percent of new breast cancer cases occur in women aged 40 and older. In the United States, the average age at breast cancer diagnosis is 61 years old.

PREGNANCY AND MENSTRUAL HISTORY: Women who have never had children, or who had their first child after age 30, are at somewhat higher risk for breast cancer. Lactation (breast feeding) may be protective against the development of breast cancer. Women who began menstruating at an early age (before 12) or continued menstruating until a later age (after 55) are also at a slightly greater risk of developing the disease. This is likely due to longer exposure to monthly cycling of the hormone *estrogen*, which can stimulate normal breast cells to divide.

ENVIRONMENTAL RISK FACTORS: Some suspected breast carcinogens include chlorinated hydrocarbons such as the pesticide DDT, which acts as an estrogen in the body, and ionizing radiation, as from nuclear power plant emissions and high-dose radiation treatment. Radiation treatment for childhood Hodgkin's lymphoma may put women at a greater risk for breast cancer later in life. While mammograms do involve exposure to radiation, the benefit from properly performed, low-dose mammography screening greatly outweighs the risk of this minimal radiation exposure.

BENIGN BREAST DISEASE: Most breast abnormalities do not represent an increased risk of breast cancer, although some represent precancerous lesions. Most fibrocystic changes, fibroadenomas and *cysts* do not increase a woman's chances of developing breast cancer. Changes called *atypia* or *hyperplasia*—changes that can only be seen by a *pathologist* as a result of a breast biopsy—can indicate an increased risk of developing breast cancer later on. *Lobular carcinoma in situ*, a precancerous lesion, is associated with a significantly increased risk of the future development of breast cancer in either breast.

HIGH BREAST TISSUE DENSITY: The higher the breast tissue density (as seen on a mammogram), the greater the risk for breast cancer. Breast tissue density is generally higher when the breast has more ducts and lobules than fat.

HORMONE REPLACEMENT THERAPY (HRT) AND ORAL CONTRACEPTIVES: There is a relationship between the hormones estrogen and *progesterone* and the risk of developing breast cancer. The Women's Health Initiative (WHI) Trial, a large, randomized U.S. trial centered at the Fred Hutchinson Cancer Research Center in Seattle, found that use of combination HRT in post-menopausal women increased the risk of breast cancer. This had been suspected based on previous studies, but the WHI study provided definitive proof. Additionally, the risk of heart disease and blood clots increased with the use of combined HRT. The same study suggested that the use of estrogen alone, without progesterone, in patients who have had a hysterectomy may not increase breast cancer risk. Progesterone is added to estrogen in women with an intact uterus to reduce the risk of uterine cancer. The results of this study have resulted in a dramatic drop in the routine use of HRT at the time of menopause in the United States, although there is undoubtedly still a role for short-term HRT use in symptomatic postmenopausal women. In women who have already been diagnosed with breast cancer, there is concern that use of supplemental estrogen will increase a woman's risk of breast cancer recurring. Some oncologists feel comfortable recommending limited use of small amounts of vaginal estrogen to decrease urogenital symptoms in breast cancer survivors.

As with postmenopausal hormones, millions of women take birth control pills (oral contraceptives) and would like to know how this may affect their risk of breast cancer. Evidence is inconclusive, although some studies suggest that current or recent use of birth control pills may slightly increase the risk of breast cancer. It is very important for every woman to weigh the pros and cons of using birth control pills before making a decision to use them. Though there are some risks associated with using the pill, it has a number of advantages as well, including preventing unwanted pregnancies and decreasing a woman's risk of both endometrial and ovarian cancers.

DIET: Obesity and high alcohol intake have been implicated in increased breast cancer risk. There may be a link between being overweight and a higher risk of breast cancer, especially for women over 50. Studies of fat in the diet as it relates to breast cancer have produced conflicting results. However, there is evidence that the disease is less common in countries where the typical diet is low in fat.

FAMILY HISTORY AND GENETICS: The risk of breast cancer is known to be higher in women whose close female relatives have had the disease, although most women diagnosed with breast cancer have no strong family history of breast cancer. This inherited risk appears to increase when multiple family members have been diagnosed with breast cancer, when family members develop breast cancer at a younger age or develop cancer in both breasts, when there is also a family history of ovarian cancer or when family members are more closely related. When looking at family history, both the maternal (mother's) and paternal (father's) sides of the family are equally important to consider.

Of all women with breast cancer, about 5 to 10 percent have a hereditary (inherited) breast cancer-associated genetic mutation. In families with inherited forms of breast cancer, there are typically more than two first-degree relatives (mother, daughters, sisters) with breast or ovarian cancer, and the disease occurs at a younger age (40s, 30s or even 20s).

Two inherited breast cancer susceptibility *genes*, BRCA1 and BRCA2, have been identified. If a parent has a mutant form of one of these genes, there is a 50 percent chance that the mutated copy of the gene will be passed on to a child. Women who inherit a mutated form of BRCA1 or BRCA2 are highly susceptible to developing breast and/or ovarian cancer—a 60 to 80 percent lifetime chance of developing breast cancer and a 15 to 30 percent chance of developing ovarian cancer. Women of Ashkenazi Jewish descent, particularly those with a family history of breast or ovarian cancer, have a higher than average risk of carrying a mutated form of the BRCA1 or BRCA2 genes. Other genes that are less commonly associated with breast cancer risk include P53, PTEN and the newly discovered CHK2 gene. Other breast cancer susceptibility genes will undoubtedly be discovered. Women can undergo genetic testing for alterations in the BRCA1 and BRCA2 genes to help determine their cancer risk—the test is done by drawing a blood sample. Usually a family member who has been diagnosed with cancer is tested first, before unaffected relatives. If a mutation in one of these genes is identified, further genetic testing can identify which family members do and do not have increased risk for cancer. A negative test for these two genes does not mean that a woman could not develop breast cancer due to other genes or risk factors. Genetic testing is expensive and is not covered by all health plans. There are also ethical, legal and social issues related to genetic testing that are best discussed before undergoing such testing. While testing the general population for mutations in BRCA1 and BRCA2 is not recommended, women with a strong family history of breast and/or ovarian cancer should be offered counseling to determine if testing is an appropriate option.

PERSONAL HISTORY OF BREAST CANCER: Having had breast cancer puts a woman at higher risk for developing it again.

Breast Cancer Risk Reduction (Prevention)

All of us would agree that, ideally, preventing breast cancer in the first place would be the best way to save lives and prevent toxic treatment. Current research on how cell changes can lead to cancer and what factors start, promote and inhibit these changes gives hope that, in the not too distant future, we will understand enough about the causes of breast cancer to prevent many cases.

Because the development of cancer is a long, multistep process, there are many ways in which it might be prevented. Avoiding or reducing exposure to *carcinogens* (cancer-causing agents) can potentially prevent the first steps that lead to cancer. Other breast cancer prevention strategies include stopping the process of cancer development after it has begun, but before the cancer manifests.

Several approaches to breast cancer prevention are currently being tested through clinical research. There are studies under way designed to evaluate dietary and lifestyle approaches to breast cancer prevention. Other studies are examining the effectiveness of *chemoprevention*—using chemicals or drugs to reduce breast cancer incidence. Because none of these approaches are likely to be 100 percent effective in "preventing" the development of cancer in all women, it is technically more correct to refer to them as breast cancer "risk reduction" strategies.

EXERCISE: Studies suggest that exercise may have a protective effect against breast cancer. Recent research has shown that women who exercise three or four hours per week at moderate to vigorous levels have a lower risk of developing the disease. Exercise may affect breast cancer risk by changing metabolic hormone levels, like insulin, and sex hormone levels, like estrogen.

DIET: General recommendations for a healthy diet that may reduce the risk of developing breast or other cancer (or prevent its *recurrence*) include the following:

- Take off excess weight (and/or prevent weight gain).

- Eat a balanced diet with a good variety of nutrients and plenty of fiber—this means plenty of fruits and vegetables!

- If you drink alcohol, do so only in moderation.

Chapter 13, Using Nutrition in the Fight Against Breast Cancer, discusses diet recommendations in more detail.

CHEMOPREVENTION: In the United States, a hormonal therapy developed for the treatment of breast cancer, *tamoxifen* (Nolvadex), has also been approved as a breast cancer chemopreventive agent. Because it was known that women who take tamoxifen for breast cancer have fewer second breast cancers, it was suspected that tamoxifen might reduce the risk of developing breast cancer for women without the disease but at a high risk. The National Surgical Breast and Bowel Project's (NSABP) P-01 Breast Cancer Prevention Trial compared breast cancer incidence in high-risk women taking tamoxifen for five years with those taking a placebo (a pill containing no medication). This study showed that women at high risk for breast cancer are about 50 percent less likely to develop the disease (at least in the short term) if they take tamoxifen. To date, although the number of breast cancers has been reduced, no improvement in overall survival has been seen in the tamoxifen group in this study.

Tamoxifen has some known toxicities, such as endometrial (uterine) cancer, blood clots, strokes, hot flashes and a watery vaginal discharge. It is believed that the benefits of tamoxifen outweigh its risks in women with a high risk of developing breast cancer, but the risks probably outweigh the benefits for women at low to moderate risk. If a woman is at high risk for breast cancer, or for developing a second breast cancer, she should discuss chemoprevention strategies such as tamoxifen with her health care provider.

Raloxifene (Evista) is a newer selective estrogen-receptor modulator (SERM), similar to tamoxifen. The major difference between tamoxifen and raloxifene is the effect on the endometrium. Raloxifene does not appear to stimulate the uterine lining and therefore should not lead to increased endometrial cancers. Raloxifene has been much less thoroughly studied with respect to breast cancer treatment and breast cancer prevention, and currently it is approved only for treating osteoporosis. The NSABP P-02 Study of Tamoxifen and Raloxifene (STAR) Trial enrolled postmenopausal women with higher than average risk of breast cancer in an attempt to compare the breast cancer prevention effects of these two drugs. Results of this trial are expected before 2008.

Ongoing clinical trials are evaluating several other classes of drugs that may reduce the risk of breast cancer. Some of these agents include *aromatase inhibitors*, drugs that function in the postmenopausal setting to reduce all remaining estrogen production. Trials comparing these agents to tamoxifen in women with breast cancer suggest that they are effective not only in reducing cancer recurrence, but also in reducing second breast cancers. The MAP-3 (EXCEL) Trial and the IBIS II Trial are two large trials evaluating the aromatase inhibitors exemestane (Aromasin) and anastrozole (Arimidex), respectively. A third potent aromatase inhibitor is letrozole (Femara).

Another interesting class of potential anticancer drugs are the COX-2 inhibitors—drugs most commonly used to treat pain and arthritis. Studies in patients with colon polyps and a high risk of developing colon cancer indicate that these drugs may have anticancer effects. Studies involving breast cancer and the COX-2 inhibitor celecoxib (Celebrex), including the S0300 Trial for premenopausal women led by the Southwest Oncology Group, are ongoing. Trials are also investigating whether aspirin and nonsteroidal anti-inflammatory drugs (NSAIDs, like ibuprofen) can decrease the risk of breast cancer occurrence.

PREVENTIVE MASTECTOMY: In some rare cases, a woman at very high risk for developing breast cancer might consider preventive *(prophylactic)* mastectomy. This is an operation in which one or both breasts are removed before there is any known breast cancer. While the operation reduces the risk of breast cancer, it is disfiguring and irreversible and can be associated with severe emotional impact. Rarely, cancer can develop in the small amount of breast tissue remaining after the operation. Breast reconstruction is usually done during the same operation. Clearly, a decision to undergo prophylactic mastectomy is something a woman should consider carefully, with the help of her health care providers.

There are many unknowns in breast cancer prevention, but we are learning more all the time. Meanwhile, we can act individually to reduce our risks through diet, exercise and avoidance of unnecessary exposure to carcinogens. Some of us can participate in clinical trials, and all of us can hope to see fewer of our family and friends stricken as we learn how to intervene in the long process that leads to breast cancer.

My life changed forever when my doctor said, "Felicia, you have breast cancer." I believed that after treatment I would never have to deal with breast cancer again, but actually that was the beginning of becoming a breast cancer survivor. I started a new phase of my life as a Cierra Sister survivor.

—*Felicia Atterberry, diagnosed in 2000 at age 31*

❧

CHAPTER 3

Screening and Diagnosis: Breast Self-Exam, Clinical Breast Exam, Mammography and Biopsy

A breast health program includes self-exam as well as working with your health care provider.

BREAST SELF-EXAM: A *breast self-exam* (BSE) begins with the pads of your fingers, not the nails. *Palpate* all the breast tissue, including the underarm area. Breasts are the least lumpy and painful at the conclusion of a menstrual cycle. If you are no longer having periods, pick a day of the month and do the exam on the same day each month. A good breast exam includes examining breasts in front of a mirror as well as while lying down. Eighty percent of all breast lumps are found by women themselves and most are not cancerous.

Some studies have suggested that BSE is unnecessary because it just makes women anxious and has not been shown to reduce the death rate from breast cancer. BSE may or may not reduce the overall death rate, but it may be important in decreasing the need for mastectomy by helping to identify cancers earlier.

An important thing to remember about BSE is to JUST DO IT! Don't be afraid of finding something or of having trouble figuring out what is normal. The more you examine your breasts over time, the more familiar you will become with their contours. Follow up with your health care provider if you discover any changes.

CLINICAL BREAST EXAM: A thorough exam by your health care provider is recommended for women at least once every three years, beginning at age 20, and annually after age 40.

MAMMOGRAPHY: Susan G. Komen for the Cure recommends the following screening guidelines for all women:

- Annual screening *mammography* for women at age 40.

- Women under 40 with either a family history of breast cancer or other concerns about their personal risk should consult with a trained medical professional about when to begin mammography.

Remember, good breast health includes all three elements: breast self-exam, clinical breast exam and mammography. This combination gives you the best possible chance of early detection of breast cancer, with the highest likelihood of cure.

Biopsy

If you discover a lump in your breast, you will want to be sure the lump or change is not breast cancer. You may need to have some, or all, of the lump removed (a *biopsy*) so that a *diagnosis* can be made by a pathologist. The pathologist will determine if the tissue removed by the biopsy is cancerous. You will probably have one of the following types of biopsies.

FINE NEEDLE ASPIRATE (FNA): A small, thin needle removes a few cells, which are placed on a slide. The pathologist will look for abnormal cells. This may not yield enough information and additional tests may be required. This procedure can be done in the doctor's office and only takes a few minutes.

CORE NEEDLE BIOPSY: A larger needle removes a small piece of tissue from the lump. The biopsy is done with local anesthesia in the doctor's office or a hospital. Ultrasound may be used to help identify the tissue to be biopsied.

STEREOTACTIC BREAST BIOPSY: This type of biopsy, guided by a special mammography machine, can direct a biopsy needle to an abnormality that is seen on the mammogram but that cannot be felt. This is done with local anesthesia in the breast center or radiology department.

SURGICAL BIOPSY: The surgeon will remove a part or all of the lump. This is scheduled as an outpatient procedure and can be done with general anesthesia, local anesthesia with sedation or local anesthesia alone.

New Breast Imaging Techniques

Mammography is the only screening method proven to reduce breast cancer mortality. However, some cancers, particularly those in women with dense breast tissue and in women at high risk for breast cancer, can be missed on mammograms. This has led scientists to investigate alternative methods of early cancer detection.

The imaging tools currently approved by the Food and Drug Administration (FDA) for diagnostic purposes (not screening) include magnetic resonance imaging (MRI), ultrasound, scintimammography, thermography and electrical impedance imaging. Of these, ultrasound plays an important role in the further evaluation of palpable or mammographic abnormalities, and MRI has an important role in defining the true extent of disease in women diagnosed with breast cancer. MRI appears to be better than ultrasound in detecting cancers early and is currently supported by several scientific organizations and many national insurance companies as a screening tool in women at high risk. Screening using MRI or ultrasound is not recommended for women at average risk of developing breast cancer.

Nautilus in the Deep

—*Anonymous Breast Cancer Survivor*

❦

Chapter 4

Dealing with a New Diagnosis of Breast Cancer

L earning that you have breast cancer can be devastating. At first, you may find it hard to control your feelings. You may feel anxious, afraid, sad or depressed. This is normal. Acknowledging your feelings and learning how to understand and manage them can help to ensure that they will not interfere with your care. Most people feel at a tremendous loss at the time of diagnosis. You may lose opportunities, your sense of yourself as a healthy person and your ability to work, if only for a time—resulting in a loss of financial security and independence. The experience of loss, whether actual or anticipated, commonly creates complex feelings of sadness, depression, anger, fear, anxiety, isolation, loneliness and guilt.

It may help to stop periodically and think about how you are feeling. Writing in a journal or talking to a trusted friend may help to clarify your emotions. Try to accept them, whatever they are. There is no right or wrong way to feel at such a difficult time. You may be inclined to keep information about your situation to yourself, not wanting to upset or burden friends and family. It is usually easier on them, however, to know what you are dealing with and how you are really feeling.

Through expressing your emotions, you will gradually become more comfortable with them and they will have less influence on your behavior. For example, talking about anger at being ill can help you to accept that cancer is something that just happened. There is no set reason for it that we can understand, no definite answer to the question, "Why me?" Sharing your thoughts with someone you trust—friend, family member or counselor—can also be very comforting. Since those closest to you may feel obligated to offer advice or solutions, you may want to explain that just listening and trying to understand are enough.

Tips for Developing Effective
Communication with Your Doctor

ॐ

- Decide what qualities you want in a doctor and seek them out.

- Always ask questions and ask for unclear information to be repeated or stated in more understandable language.

- Write your questions down ahead of time and make sure that all of them are answered. You may want to request descriptions of tests or treatments, information on their benefits and risks, which are recommended and why and any relevant insurance issues. Ask for another appointment if you need more time. Getting your questions answered can add to your sense of control.

- Keep a written record of meetings with your doctors. Include the names of your care team, medications and dosages, dates of tests, upcoming appointments and so on. You will be receiving a great deal of important information and may find that you need an organizing system to keep track of it all. Some drug companies produce treatment planners and guides, and many larger treatment facilities provide patient notebooks designed for this purpose. Ask your care team about resources that may be available to you. Local book and stationary stores also carry planners that can easily be adapted.

- Take someone with you to your appointments to be your note taker, or tape-record the discussion for later review. One person usually cannot hear and absorb all that is said.

- If communication with your doctor is difficult, let him or her know. If this is not comfortable for you, tell another member of your care team whom you find more approachable. That person may be able to help clear up any misunderstandings or suggest strategies for communicating more effectively.

- If communication is still a problem, you may want to consider changing doctors. It is important to find a doctor with whom you can communicate well as you enter the treatment process.

Maintain a Positive Attitude

Many patients have said that the period before they began treatment was the most difficult. Once you actually start treatment, you may feel better. You begin to get comfortable with your health care team and to make connections with other patients who are being treated at the same time. Also, by this time, you probably will have learned about potential problems related to your treatment. You begin to see what the treatment is like and how you are reacting to it, which can help you to feel more in control.

Because each patient is unique, reactions to treatment—even the same treatment—can vary widely. Some patients have little trouble, while others may experience several problems. You can minimize problems by keeping your medical caregivers informed of any changes or concerns and by keeping yourself in the best condition possible. Adequate sleep, good nutrition and appropriate exercise have never been more important. Taking care of yourself emotionally is essential too. Try to think positively. You may not be able to choose your reality, but you can choose how to think about and respond to it. Do you see yourself as a helpless victim or as a fighter with a powerful team of doctors, family and friends supporting you? The way you choose to define your situation can have a powerful effect on your outlook.

Thinking positively does not mean ignoring potential threats and dangers; it means choosing not to focus on the negative aspects of your situation. Focus instead on the reasons you can feel hopeful about your treatment, the knowledge and special skills of your physicians, the support of your family, the good things in your life that you can appreciate right now, your strengths and your success in solving other problems in your life.

Some patients turn to spiritual beliefs and prayer to maintain a positive outlook. Others find that relaxation techniques or meditation are powerful tools for regaining focus after the unsettling news of a cancer diagnosis. Taking a positive approach to situations that arise during your day-to-day treatment can also contribute to your overall sense of control. And, as with all medical concerns, it is a good idea to try to anticipate problems that may occur.

Take an Active Role in Your Treatment

Research suggests that people who take an active role in their care and make their own decisions adjust better to major challenges, such as a diagnosis of breast cancer.

Begin by establishing good relationships with your health care providers. While we tend to assume that all doctors are experienced, attentive, kindly and caring human beings, like any other group of individuals, doctors can be jerks or jewels. And, as in any relationship, communication between patients and their doctors involves give and take. Under the best circumstances, the communication process evolves into a mutual partnership. Most patients want, at least in part, to make their own care decisions. If this is true for you, let your doctor know that you expect to be an active member of your medical team.

Take Charge of Making Treatment Decisions

Every woman has her own decision-making style. Some rely primarily on logic and reason, others on feelings and intuition. Some women make decisions quickly, while others need a lot of time to evaluate their options. You may want to simply write down your options, listing the pros and cons of each. If you are naturally intuitive, you may find that meditation, prayer or drawing appeal more to you. Talking to a neutral friend or resource person can also help.

It is natural to feel fearful or uncertain about upcoming surgery, radiation treatment or chemotherapy. If you research and review all of your options thoroughly, when you do decide on a treatment you will have more confidence as you go forward. No matter how you finally come to your treatment decision, it is most important to choose the course that is right for you. Then stand firmly behind it. Your fears and uncertainties will diminish and you will be able to turn your attention to making the treatment work.

Get up some courage
Take a deep breath, get ready
Get ready to jump

—*Susan Sutley*

CHAPTER 5

Before Treatment Begins: Staging, Lab Tests and Second Opinions

Staging

Breast cancer is a disease in which cells in normal breast tissue become *malignant*, growing and spreading uncontrollably. Breasts are composed of *lobules*, which are connected by thin tubes called ducts. The most common type of breast cancer is *infiltrating ductal cancer*. It is found in the cells of the ducts. Cancer that begins in the lobules is called *infiltrating lobular cancer*. Lobular cancer is more often found in both breasts (bilaterally) than other types of breast cancer.

The *stage* of breast cancer is a measure at diagnosis of the extent of cancer involvement and where the cancer is located (within the breast, *lymph nodes* or the rest of the body). With the increasing use of screening mammograms, breast cancers are now diagnosed at earlier stages than previously.

THE STAGE OF A BREAST CANCER REFLECTS:

- *Tumor* size
- Lymph node involvement (whether there is spread through the *lymphatic system* within the breast to the regional lymph nodes)
- Local spread (whether there is spread to neighboring structures like the skin or chest wall)

- Distant spread (whether there is *metastasis,* or spread to distant organs like the lungs, liver or bones, which generally occurs through the lymphatics or bloodstream)

CARCINOMA IN SITU: Stage 0. An abnormal growth of cells that stays within the area in which it started and does not spread is called *carcinoma in situ.* About 15 to 20 percent of breast cancers are in situ, or noninvasive. Because it is entirely surrounded by the wall of the duct or lobule, noninvasive breast cancer does not grow into the rest of the breast tissue, does not have access to blood vessels or lymphatics and therefore does not spread beyond the breast itself.

There are two types of breast cancer in situ. *Ductal carcinoma in situ* (DCIS, also known as *intraductal* carcinoma) arises from the ducts. DCIS is thought to have the potential to develop into an invasive cancer, so it must be treated. *Lobular carcinoma in situ* (LCIS) is not cancer, but for purposes of classifying the disease it is called breast cancer in situ. Patients with LCIS have a 25 percent chance of developing breast cancer in either breast within twenty-five years. The usual recommendation for women with LCIS is close monitoring and screening.

EARLY INVASIVE BREAST CANCER: Stages I and II. More than 50 percent of women with invasive breast cancer have Stage I disease at diagnosis (a tumor size of 2 centimeters or smaller, without spread to lymph nodes). Another 15 to 20 percent have Stage II disease at diagnosis (2 cm or smaller with limited lymph node involvement, greater than 2 cm and less than 5 cm with or without limited lymph node involvement, or greater than 5 cm without lymph node involvement). These are often referred to as early breast cancers.

ADVANCED INVASIVE BREAST CANCER: Stage III. The new staging system classifies patients with four or more involved lymph nodes as having a Stage III (locally advanced) disease. Stage III also includes patients with involvement of the skin or chest wall. Inflammatory breast cancer is classified as Stage IIIB. It is an uncommon type of cancer in which the breast is warm, red and swollen due to the invasion of the tumor into the lymphatics of the skin.

Stage IV Breast Cancer: Refers to cancer that has spread beyond the breast and regional lymph nodes. Occasionally, cancer has spread beyond the breast and lymph nodes at the time of diagnosis. More commonly, Stage IV disease is diagnosed months to years after the original breast cancer. The bones, liver, lungs and more distant lymph nodes can be sites of metastatic breast cancer recurrence. In Stage IV disease, the treatment focus is on the other sites of disease, and not usually the breast or lymph nodes. Since

Stage IV cancer cannot be cured, the goal of treatment for Stage IV disease is management of the cancer so the patient can live comfortably with the cancer. As treatments are improving, patients are living longer and feeling better despite Stage IV breast cancer.

Special Laboratory Tests

HORMONE-RECEPTOR TESTS: Such tests for estrogen and progesterone receptors are done on breast cancer tissue removed during biopsy or surgery to help determine *prognosis* and predict whether the cancer is sensitive to hormone therapy. When the hormones estrogen and progesterone attach to these receptors found in normal breast cells or breast cancer cells, they send a series of signals that can stimulate the cells to grow and divide.

Hormone-receptor tests help physicians decide whether endocrine (hormone) therapy or chemotherapy may be useful for a given patient. Positive test results mean that the cancer is more likely to respond to endocrine treatment, such as the anti-estrogen drug tamoxifen (Nolvadex), or to decreasing the level of estrogen in the body using drugs called aromatase inhibitors (anastrazole, letrozole or exemestane). Tumors that have hormone receptors are generally associated with a more favorable prognosis.

Paradoxically, breast cancers in postmenopausal women are more likely to have positive hormone receptors than are those in premenopausal women.

OTHER TESTS: Other tests on breast cancer tissue are sometimes done to help predict whether the tumor is likely to grow slowly or quickly, whether it is likely to recur and which treatments are likely to be effective. These tests might include oncogene or tumor suppressor gene tests, which look for mutations in cancer-related genes and proteins, including *HER-2* and p53. Measurements of cell proliferation or DNA content may include Ki67, S-phase and DNA index tests.

TUMOR GRADE: Tumor *grade* is frequently evaluated on the biopsy or surgical specimen and noted on the pathology report. Several grading systems for breast cancer exist, including the Nottingham and Bloom-Richardson scales. In general, low-grade tumors have less aggressive features and are less likely to recur distantly, compared to high-grade tumors.

TUMOR MARKERS: These *markers* are substances that can be detected in higher than normal amounts in blood, urine or body tissues of some patients with cancer. Tumor marker tests that may be done on a breast cancer patient's blood include CEA and CA 27.29 (also called CA 15.3). These tests are usually only positive in bulky or advanced breast cancer disease and therefore cannot be used for diagnosis or early detection. However, tumor markers may be used to follow the course of the disease, to determine the effect of treatment and to check for recurrence. The usefulness of obtaining each test will be determined by the treating physicians.

Potential Treatment Options

Many treatment methods are used for breast cancer. The treatment for an individual patient depends on several factors, including the following:

- The type of cancer
- The size and location of the tumor in the breast
- The mammogram or other imaging findings (such as ultrasound or MRI)
- The results of lab tests done on cancer cells (including hormone receptors)
- The stage (or extent) of disease
- Patient factors (health status, menopausal status, treatment preferences, etc)

This list explains why two patients with seemingly similar diagnoses may receive different treatment recommendations. Treatment may also be influenced by further tests to determine whether the cancer has spread. A chest X-ray and blood tests to check the liver are standard in invasive disease. In more advanced stages, bone scans or computed tomography (CT) scans of the lungs or liver may be indicated, since breast cancer can spread to these areas.

FOR DCIS: Treatment is focused on the area of the breast and includes surgery with or without radiation therapy. The main goal is preventing a local recurrence in the breast or chest tissue. Some women with DCIS may benefit from taking the medication tamoxifen to reduce the risk of developing a breast cancer recurrence or second breast cancer.

FOR STAGES I AND II: The initial treatment is usually surgery. If breast conservation (lumpectomy) is being done, surgery is usually followed by radiation therapy. Chemotherapy and/or endocrine therapy are also usually recommended. The sequence of surgery and systemic therapy (endocrine and/or chemotherapy) has traditionally involved surgery prior to systemic therapy. However, several studies have shown that it is safe to take systemic therapy before or after surgery. Treatment given before surgery is called *neo-adjuvant* or *primary systemic therapy*.

FOR STAGE III: Treatment may start with either surgery or total body treatment (neoadjuvant chemotherapy or sometimes endocrine therapy), followed by surgery and usually radiation.

Systemic treatment is aimed at reducing the likelihood of tumor spread in the future and at increasing the possibility of cure. This adjuvant treatment (meaning "in addition to") is supplemental to the local treatment with surgery and/or radiation therapy. It may include chemotherapy, endocrine therapy or both. Adjuvant treatment does not guarantee that distant spread of cancer will not occur in the future, but it does lower the likelihood.

FOR STAGE IV: There are a wide range of treatments for Stage IV breast cancer, depending upon sites of spread, features of the tumor (such as hormone receptors) and the age, menopausal status and general health of the patient. Stage IV breast cancer is generally viewed as an incurable disease, although there is wide variation in the number of years that patients may live with the disease, and there is optimism that some women may be cured with new forms of treatment.

Second Opinions

Most physicians will support a patient's efforts to obtain more information, including a *second opinion*, especially in making early decisions about breast cancer therapy. Many insurance companies will cover a second opinion regarding surgery. It may be advisable and helpful to include a *radiation oncologist* and a medical oncologist as consultants early in the treatment planning, in addition to a surgeon.

I really appreciated those who were working in this field—nurses, doctors, researchers, and all other workers, especially Veronica who is all the time working so hard for breast cancer support within the Korean community. I didn't know anything about breast cancer, but I learned a lot of breast health information, prevention, and breast self examination (BSE) through her workshop. Now I encourage my friends to do BSE and annual breast exams with a mammogram. I enjoy my second life; "thank you," to all who saved my life.

—Jeon Ja Lee, diagnosed in 1993 at age 49

Surgery for Breast Cancer: Mastectomy versus Lumpectomy, Axillary Lymph Node Evaluation, Reconstruction

Breast Surgery

Surgery is the most common initial treatment for breast cancer. An operation to remove the breast is called *mastectomy*. An operation to remove the cancer but not the breast is called *lumpectomy*, breast-sparing surgery, breast conservation or local excision.

In a total (or simple) mastectomy, the surgeon removes the entire breast. In a *modified radical mastectomy,* the surgeon removes the breast and most of the lower and middle lymph nodes in the armpit.

The goal in breast-sparing surgery is to remove the cancer surrounded by a rim of normal tissue, to obtain clean *margins.* Breast-sparing surgery is usually followed by radiation therapy to destroy any cancer cells that may remain in the breast and to reduce the risk of cancer recurring.

For appropriately selected patients, women undergoing mastectomy do not necessarily live longer than those treated with breast conservation and radiation therapy. In other words, mastectomy does not guarantee longer survival than lumpectomy and radiation. The 1990 National Institutes of Health (NIH) Consensus Conference on the Treatment of Early Stage Breast Cancer concluded that "breast conservation treatment is an appropriate method of primary therapy for the majority of women with Stage I and II breast cancer and is preferable because it provides survival equivalent to mastectomy while preserving the breast."

THE DECISION BETWEEN MASTECTOMY AND BREAST CONSERVATION DEPENDS ON MANY FACTORS, INCLUDING THE FOLLOWING:

- The patient's preference
- The size of the tumor
- The location of the tumor within the breast
- The size of the breast
- The presence of DCIS, LCIS, atypia or hyperplasia
- The likelihood that all of the tumor can be removed without removing the entire breast
- The presence of *microcalcifications* on the mammogram
- The anticipated cosmetic result
- The ability to adequately monitor the patient for recurrences after surgery
- The patient's age and health
- A history of connective tissue disorders, like scleroderma or lupus
- The location of the nearest radiation facility
- Previous treatment with radiation for lymphoma or other medical conditions
- Pregnancy (first or second trimester)

Some women who are not initially candidates for breast conservation may benefit from being treated with chemotherapy and/or radiation therapy before surgery. If the tumor shrinks significantly, they may then be able to have breast conservation surgery.

Lymph Node Evaluation

In most cases of invasive breast cancer and some cases of DCIS, the surgeon also recommends evaluation of the lymph nodes under the arm to help determine the stage of disease, remove all of the cancer and plan further treatment. The standard *axillary lymph node dissection* removes all the lymphatic tissue below the large vein in the armpit area (Level I and II nodes). *Sentinel lymph node biopsy* is a newer procedure that allows selected patients to have fewer lymph nodes removed.

Surgical Treatment Questions to Ask Your Surgeon

ॐ

- How much breast surgery do you perform in your practice?

- Do I have a choice between breast conservation and mastectomy? Do you recommend one over the other for my particular circumstances? Why?

- If I have a mastectomy and am interested in reconstruction, is it better to have it delayed or can I have it at the time of the mastectomy?

- Am I a candidate for sentinel lymph node biopsy? What is your experience in doing this procedure?

The sentinel lymph node is the first lymph node or nodes in the chain of nodes that drains the area of the cancer. They are identified by using a radioactive isotope marker substance and/or blue dye injected around the tumor or near the nipple. The marker and dye travel through the lymphatic channels and collect in the sentinel lymph node(s). A special camera may be used to take pictures of the location of the sentinel lymph node preoperatively.

During surgery the blue dye can be seen, and the lymph node radioactivity can be identified by a handheld isotope counter. Usually an initial pathology test of the sentinel lymph node is done during surgery. If no cancer is identified in the sentinel lymph node, then no more lymph nodes are removed. Further testing is done on the sentinel lymph node, and results may take several days. If these tests do not show any cancer cells in the lymph nodes then no further lymph node surgery is necessary. If the sentinel lymph nodes have cancer in them on these tests, another operation may be recommended to remove more of the lymph nodes in the armpit because other nodes may have cancer cells in them too.

Breast Reconstruction Surgery

Breast reconstruction is an option for some patients who have had mastectomies. The decision to have reconstruction is an individual woman's choice. Many factors play into making this decision, and psychosocial support is available to help women with it. Reconstruction may be started at the time of the mastectomy (immediate reconstruction) or may be done six months or longer after the mastectomy (delayed reconstruction). Reconstruction typically involves either the insertion of an *implant* or a *tissue flap transfer*.

BREAST IMPLANTS: Breast implants are plastic sacs filled with either *silicone* (a type of plastic liquid) or saline (salt water) that are surgically placed behind the chest muscles. Silicone implants are used less frequently than saline, but appear to be safe. In November, 2006, the U.S. Food and Drug Administration (FDA) lifted a moratorium on silicone-filled implants for women 22 years old and older and for post-mastectomy women of all ages. Follow-up studies for the safety and effectiveness of the implants is a condition for its approval, as questions still remain about whether leaking silicone could lead to diseases. Susan G. Komen for the Cure continues to support the availability of silicone breast implants as an option for women considering reconstructive surgery due to mastectomy. Patients should be informed of risks associated with silicone breast implants and discuss these risks with a plastic surgeon in order to select the choice that is best for them.

IMPLANTS HAVE BEEN ASSOCIATED WITH THE FOLLOWING RISKS:

- Capsular contracture (hardening of the breast reconstruction because of scar tissue)
- Leaking and/or rupturing
- Calcium deposits in surrounding tissue
- Shifting from the original placement site
- Infection

Women considering breast implants should discuss these issues with their plastic surgeon and may want to contact the FDA for its most recent opinion on these devices.

TISSUE TRANSPLANTS OR FLAPS: This method involves taking muscle, fat and skin from another part of the body and moving it to the chest area, where it is shaped into the form of a breast. Tissue is usually taken from either the lower stomach (the transverse rectus abdominis myocutaneous

Reconstruction-Related
Questions to Ask Your Surgeon

SELECTING A PLASTIC SURGEON

☐ How many breast reconstructions (implants and/or tissue transplants) have you done?

☐ May I see pictures of your patients who have had reconstruction?

☐ Can you put me in contact with someone who has had the procedure?

UNDERSTANDING RECONSTRUCTION

☐ What are the various types of reconstructive surgery?

☐ What are the risks and potential side effects from each type? Will detection of a possible recurrence be difficult? Will there be pain? Will I need a special bra?

☐ What can I expect the reconstruction to look and feel like? Will it be similar in look and feel to my healthy breast? Will there be differences over time: in three months, six months, a year? Will I have anything done to the healthy breast?

☐ What type of reconstruction is best for me? Why?

☐ When is the best time for me to have reconstruction: immediately after the mastectomy, or later, after chemotherapy and/or radiation therapy? What are the advantages to immediate reconstruction? What are the advantages to delayed reconstruction?

☐ How many procedures will it take? How long will it take? Where will these procedures be performed? How much time will recovery take?

☐ Will my insurance cover this type of surgery?

flap, or *TRAM flap)* or the back (the latissimus dorsi muscle, or *lat flap)*. Another, less commonly used, option is to take tissue from the buttocks (the gluteus muscle). The TRAM flap is the one most commonly used for breast reconstruction, but it is not appropriate for all women. These are all major surgeries involving large wounds, significant recovery periods and potential surgical complications such as poor wound healing and infections. Although there are definitely risks to these surgical procedures, many women report physical and emotional satisfaction from tissue flap breast reconstruction.

≥❧

The choice of procedure may be limited by the patient's medical history, previous abdominal surgeries, body build, prior radiation therapy and smoking history. For a woman contemplating a mastectomy where reconstruction may be a consideration, a consultation with a plastic surgeon prior to mastectomy is advisable. Ask your breast surgeon for a referral to an experienced plastic surgeon or use a referral from the American Society of Plastic and Reconstructive Surgeons.

Breast reconstruction is a process that often takes several months to complete. Frequently, surgery may be recommended on the other breast to make it more symmetrical with the reconstructed breast. Washington State law requires health insurers to pay for reconstruction of the removed breast and/or surgery on the nondiseased breast to make it equal in size and contour. Medicare and Medicaid are required to pay for reconstruction.

There are information guides available that list questions to help you decide whether or not you want reconstructive surgery, what kind of reconstruction and by whom. In addition, some surgeons have support and/or information exchange groups where women are encouraged to share information, observations, emotions and experiences. Inquire into these.

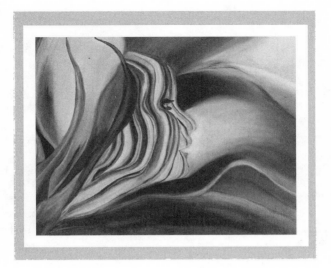

—*Joan Rodriguiz, Breast Cancer Survivor*

❦

CHAPTER 7

Radiation Therapy

R*adiation therapy* uses X-rays to kill breast cancer cells. Radiation therapy is often used in combination with surgery for early stage breast cancer. In most cases, a lumpectomy is followed by radiation therapy, to reduce the risk of local recurrence of the breast cancer within the remaining tissue. In some cases, radiation is also recommended following a mastectomy if there is a high risk of tumor cells remaining behind after surgery. This includes tumors extending to the edge of the surgery specimen, tumors close to the rib cage or chest wall muscles, very large tumors (greater than 5 cm) or when several lymph nodes are involved.

HOW RADIATION IS DELIVERED: When radiation therapy follows breast surgery, a machine delivers radiation to the breast/chest wall and in some cases to the regional lymph nodes. This is called external beam radiation. The treatments are generally given five days a week for six to seven weeks. Each treatment takes a few minutes. At the end of the series of treatments, an extra boost of radiation is sometimes given to the area where the cancer was found. During the actual radiation treatment, you will be alone in a room, but your radiation therapist will be able to hear and see you. You cannot see or feel anything while the equipment is in operation; however, you can hear the machine being turned on and off.

A slightly longer initial radiation therapy visit, called a simulation, is required to determine the exact area to be radiated (called the radiation *port*) and the setup of the radiation machine. Tiny permanent skin tattoos or ink, and a cast or mold to keep the arm in the same position above the head, are generally used to assure that the radiation port is identical for each treatment.

For patients with metastatic breast cancer, radiation may be used to treat an area where cancer has spread. For example, if breast cancer has spread to the bones and is causing pain, radiation to the affected bone may lessen the pain.

SIDE EFFECTS: Possible *side effects* of radiation include fatigue and skin irritation, such as itchiness, redness, soreness, peeling or darkening of the breast. Other, less common radiation side effects in breast cancer patients can include radiation pneumonitis (inflammation of the lung tissue) or rib fractures. Radiation to the breast does not cause hair loss, vomiting or diarrhea. Most side effects that arise during the course of radiation therapy will subside after the treatments have been completed. You are not radioactive during or after your therapy.

PARTIAL BREAST RADIATION: An experimental technique for breast radiation currently under investigation is called partial breast radiation. This type of radiation focuses on only part of the breast tissue, the area around the lumpectomy site. Usually, more intensive radiation is delivered over a shorter time period compared to standard external beam radiation. Most partial breast radiation treatments are completed in about five days.

BRACHYTHERAPY: This is a type of partial breast radiation that is internal. There are several different techniques for brachytherapy, including a balloon that can be inserted in the operating room to deliver radiation, radiation seeds that are implanted into the breast and external catheters that can be temporarily placed around the lumpectomy scar and hooked up one to two times a day to deliver focused radiation.

Partial breast radiation has not yet been proven to be as effective as conventional external beam radiation therapy and should be performed only in the setting of a clinical trial. The National Surgical Breast and Bowel Project's (NSABP) large, randomized national clinical trial (B-39/RTOG 0413) started enrollment in early 2006. It will compare conventional whole breast radiation to experimental partial breast radiation in selected women with Stages 0 to II breast cancer.

My husband and I came to the U.S. from China in 1968. When I found a lump during a breast self exam and was diagnosed with breast cancer, I underwent a lumpectomy followed by radiation treatments. I have joined Angel Care Breast Cancer Foundation. Our goal is to reach out and help those newly diagnosed with breast cancer. I've learned from Angel Care that a positive attitude *does* make a difference in our lives. One of my two daughters is expecting, and I look forward to holding my first grandchild soon.

—*Jean Chang, diagnosed in 1998 at age 56*

CHAPTER 8

೪

Systemic Therapy for Breast Cancer

Surgery and radiation therapy are powerful ways of eradicating cancer within the breast and the adjacent lymph nodes. Many breast cancer patients are cured by surgery alone (with or without radiation therapy). Both surgery and radiation are considered "local" therapies because they have no effect on cancer cells that may have spread. In breast cancer, even when the tumor is small, cancer cells may have already spread beyond the breast. Unfortunately, some patients develop recurrence of breast cancer in distant sites (including the liver, bones and lungs). This can occur within months of the original diagnosis or many years later.

Therapies that circulate through the body's bloodstream to attack cancer cells wherever they may have spread are called systemic therapies. Systemic therapies can be used in early stage breast cancer patients after breast surgery to reduce the risk of later recurrence. This is called *adjuvant therapy* (meaning "in addition to"). Treatment given before breast surgery is called *neoadjuvant therapy*. Systemic therapies are also used as metastatic treatment in patients with evidence of distant cancer spread (Stage IV cancer) to shrink the cancer and prolong survival. If a patient's cancer presents or recurs in distant sites in the body, then systemic therapy is generally used as the primary treatment. Help in killing distant cancer cells comes from *endocrine therapy*, *chemotherapy* and the newer drug class called *biologic* or *targeted therapy*.

Adjuvant and Neoadjuvant Therapy

Not all patients who are diagnosed with early stage breast cancer receive systemic therapy. Many factors are taken into consideration when a treatment plan is being decided. Since the purpose of adjuvant treatment is to prevent a cancer recurrence, an individualized assessment of a patient's cancer recurrence risk must be made. Patient preference for treatment may also play an important role, especially in situations in which survival rates are similar for different treatment options, or the benefit from adding systemic therapy is small. The patient's age, menopausal status, health and lifestyle must be taken into account.

Even the most sensitive blood tests and radiologic scans cannot detect small numbers of circulating breast cancer cells at an early stage, when distant breast cancer is most curable. As a result, recommendations for adjuvant therapy must be based on estimating the chance that a patient's tumor cells have already spread through the bloodstream or the lymphatic system to a distant site, the stage of the tumor (size, lymph node status and evidence of distant spread) and the hormone receptor status of the tumor (estrogen and progesterone receptors). The pathologic grade of the tumor, DNA studies (ploidy, S-phase) and some oncogene studies (HER-2) may also influence the decision about whether or not a patient may benefit from systemic therapy.

Neoadjuvant (preoperative) therapy is most commonly recommended to reduce the size of the cancer so that it is easier to remove during surgery, or easier to treat with radiation. In some cases, neoadjuvant therapy may reduce the tumor size so that it is small enough to allow for breast-conserving surgery (lumpectomy) instead of mastectomy.

The decision about whether to include chemotherapy, endocrine therapy or biologic therapy in a patient's breast cancer treatment plan must weigh the possible benefits to be gained from the treatment with the risks and side effects of that treatment. The possible benefits are a reduction in the likelihood of recurrence at a later time and a decrease in the chance of dying from breast cancer. The risks and side effects will vary depending on the drugs, and are discussed below.

METASTATIC (STAGE IV) TREATMENT: Goals in the treatment of advanced breast cancer include a shrinkage or *remission* of the cancer, a slowing or delay in cancer progression, an improvement in cancer-related symptoms and a prolongation of survival. Surgery and/or radiation therapy are occasionally used in the treatment of metastatic breast cancer, but because breast cancer rarely recurs in only one site, systemic therapy is the mainstay of metastatic breast cancer treatment.

Most new drugs are first tested in clinical trials in patients with metastatic breast cancer, and then, if effective and safe, tested in earlier stage breast cancer. Because cure is rare in Stage IV breast cancer, considering participation in a clinical trial of a new drug or treatment strategy is always a reasonable option. For patients with breast cancer recurrence in the bones, the most common site of distant spread, a class of drugs called *bisphosphonates* that inhibit bone breakdown are usually added to other anticancer drugs (see the discussion of bisphosphonates later this chapter).

Endocrine Therapy

Endocrine or hormonal treatment for breast cancer is used to block the effect of estrogen or to reduce estrogen levels. Some breast cancers need estrogen and/or progesterone to grow. About two-thirds of women with breast cancer have tumors that contain estrogen or progesterone receptors, and these are the cancers that can potentially benefit from endocrine treatment. Like chemotherapy, endocrine therapy is a systemic treatment that can affect cancer cells throughout the body.

Estrogen production is different in premenopausal and postmenopausal women. In premenopausal women, estrogen production occurs mainly in the ovaries. In postmenopausal women, estrogen levels are much lower, and most estrogen production occurs in other body tissues. There are various types of endocrine treatments available, depending on menopausal status.

AROMATASE INHIBITORS: This class of oral endocrine treatments, effective only in postmenopausal women, works by lowering estrogen levels in the body. Hormones called androgens are made by the adrenal gland and changed into estrogen by an enzyme called aromatase. An aromatase inhibitor is a drug that blocks aromatase. Before menopause, the ovaries make most of the estrogen in the body, but postmenopausally, most of the remaining estrogen is made through the aromatase enzyme.

Anastrozole (Arimidex), letrozole (Femara) and exemestane (Aromasin) are aromatase inhibitors approved for the treatment of breast cancer. Aromatase inhibitors are effective for treatment of metastatic breast cancer. Clinical trials within the past five years have demonstrated the effectiveness of these drugs in the adjuvant setting, either instead of tamoxifen or following tamoxifen. Several large clinical trials suggest that aromatase inhibitors may reduce the risk of breast cancer recurrence more effectively than tamoxifen alone in postmenopausal women.

When used as adjuvant treatment for early stage breast cancer, the optimal treatment period for aromatase inhibitors is not known. These drugs are currently under investigation as breast cancer chemoprevention agents.

Some of the most common side effects associated with the use of aromatase inhibitors include hot flashes, joint problems, effects on bones (including fractures and bone density) and effects on cholesterol.

ANTI-ESTROGENS: Tamoxifen (Nolvadex), another oral agent, was until recently the most commonly used form of endocrine therapy in both adjuvant and metastatic treatment. It is in a class of endocrine therapies called selective estrogen-receptor modulators (SERMs). It acts as an *anti-estrogen,* or a hormone blocker, on breast tissue and some breast cancers, but can act as a weak estrogen on some other tissues. It works by binding to the estrogen receptor and preventing estrogen's ability to stimulate growth of the tumor cell.

Tamoxifen is an effective metastatic and adjuvant treatment for breast cancer, in both pre- and postmenopausal women. In the adjuvant setting, five years appears to be an optimal treatment duration. Although adjuvant aromatase inhibitors have shown a small reduction in recurrences when compared to tamoxifen in recent clinical trials in postmenopausal women, tamoxifen is still the preferred endocrine treatment for premenopausal women. Tamoxifen is also the only drug approved for the prevention of breast cancer, reducing the diagnosis of breast cancer by 40 to 50 percent when compared to a placebo in large clinical chemoprevention trials.

Side effects include hot flashes, nausea, weight gain and depression. Studies show that there is a slight increased risk of uterine (endometrial) cancer and blood clots for women on this drug, although these are quite rare. Women taking tamoxifen should have an annual pelvic exam and notify their doctor of any unusual vaginal bleeding. Tamoxifen can help prevent thinning of the bones (osteoporosis) and decrease the risk of heart attacks.

Toremifene (Fareston) and raloxifene (Evista) are also SERMs. Toremifene is approved by the Food and Drug Administration (FDA) for use in metastatic breast cancer and is very similar to tamoxifen. Raloxifene has been approved for prevention of osteoporosis and is being investigated in breast cancer prevention.

Fulvestrant (faslodex) is in another class of anti-estrogen treatments called selective estrogen-receptor downregulators (SERDs). In contrast to the oral aromatase inhibitors and SERMs, fulvestrant is given as a monthly intramuscular injection. It is currently approved for the treatment of advanced breast cancer and is under investigation in earlier stage breast cancer. Because it is a "pure" anti-estrogen, all of its side effects relate to estrogen repression.

OVARIAN SUPPRESSION: One approach to the treatment of hormone receptor–positive breast cancer in premenopausal women is to make the ovaries stop producing estrogen. This can be achieved by removing the ovaries (oophorectomy), radiating the ovaries or using a luteinizing hormone-releasing hormone (LHRH) agonist. Additionally, cancer chemotherapy frequently suppresses ovarian hormone production. The benefits of ovarian suppression (as well as the addition of aromatase inhibitors) in premenopausal women with early stage breast cancer are currently under investigation in two large international trials, the Suppression of Ovarian Function Trial (SOFT) and the Tamoxifen and Exemestane Trial (TEST).

Chemotherapy

Chemotherapy is the use of drugs to kill cancer cells and improve a patient's chance of cure. Chemotherapy may be given by mouth or by injection into a vein or muscle. The drugs then enter the bloodstream and travel through the body to attack cancer cells that may have spread from the original site. Adjuvant chemotherapy has been proven through large clinical trials to improve the cure rate and overall survival for breast cancer patients. Adjuvant chemotherapy may reduce the risk of recurrence in breast cancer patients by as much as 40 percent.

Drugs used in chemotherapy are called cytotoxic drugs because they kill cells. The drugs circulate throughout the body in the bloodstream and may kill any rapidly growing cells, including cancer cells and some healthy cells. Chemotherapy drugs are carefully controlled in both dosage and frequency so that cancer cells are destroyed while minimizing the effects on healthy cells. Most patients undergoing chemotherapy for breast cancer are treated on an outpatient basis in a hospital or clinic, where nurses and pharmacists are specially trained and certified in cancer treatment.

Chemotherapy for breast cancer is not all the same. There are different drugs and also different recipes (or regimens) using combinations of drugs. The best results in the adjuvant treatment of breast cancer are usually obtained when several drugs are used together, known as *combination chemotherapy*. Chemotherapy is given in cycles—a treatment period followed by a recovery period, then another treatment. Most current adjuvant breast cancer chemotherapy regimens include anywhere from four to eight cycles of treatment, with regimens lasting between three and six months. The most common treatment regimens include combinations of one or more of the following drugs: doxorubicin (Adriamycin), methotrexate, 5-fluoro-uracil (5-FU), cyclophosphamide (Cytoxan), paclitaxel (Taxol) or docetaxel (Taxotere).

In a recent trial of Adriamycin—the Cancer and Leukemia Group B (CALGB) 9741 Trial—Cytoxan and Taxol given to early stage breast cancer patients in treatment intervals that were either conventional (every three weeks) or dose dense (every two weeks, with growth factors) resulted in fewer recurrences and deaths for the women who received dose-dense treatment. A large, ongoing national clinical trial—Southwest Oncology Group (SWOG) S0221—is currently comparing the dose-dense treatment approach to a regimen developed at the University of Washington called metronomic dosing. Metronomic dosing refers to lower, more frequent doses of chemotherapy drugs, the goal being to achieve more constant chemotherapy exposure to the cancer cell, with potentially fewer side effects. It is also hypothesized that metronomic dosing may prevent the tumor's supply of blood vessels from developing (angiogenesis inhibition), which could also result in more anticancer effectiveness.

For patients with metastatic or recurrent disease, there are many other effective chemotherapy drugs as well. All of the drugs used in the adjuvant setting have efficacy in advanced breast cancer. The taxanes are probably the most effective. Other effective chemotherapy drugs include capecitabine (Xeloda), vinorelbine (Navelbine) and gemcitabine (Gemzar). In an attempt to decrease toxicity and improve efficacy, novel formulations of two common breast cancer drugs have been developed: liposomal doxorubicin (Doxil) and albumin-bound-paclitaxel (Abraxane).

SIDE EFFECTS: All adjuvant chemotherapy regimens for breast cancer cause side effects, but most patients are able to do their usual activities most of the time (at a slower pace). Fatigue is the most common side effect and often is worse near the end of treatment. Studies show that mild exercise can decrease the symptoms of fatigue. Many women treated for breast cancer experience some nausea. New, improved antinausea medications may be prescribed in those cases.

The blood cells that are made in the *bone marrow* (white blood cells that fight infection, *red blood cells* that carry oxygen and *platelets* that help stop bleeding) can all be affected by the chemotherapy drugs. Levels of these blood cells are checked frequently while patients are receiving chemotherapy. Low levels of certain cells may lead to changes in chemotherapy doses, blood transfusions and/or the addition of blood cell growth factors.

Growth factors are frequently used to help boost the numbers of white cells (neutrophils) or red cells. White blood cell growth factors include filgrastim (Neupogen, G-CSF) and the longer-acting pegfilgrastim (Neulasta). Red blood cell growth factors include epoetin alfa (Procrit, Epo) and darbepoetin alfa (Aranesp).

Hair loss *(alopecia)*, skin and nail changes, changes in bowel movements, interruption of menstrual cycles, infections, a tingling or numbing sensation of the hands or feet and mouth sores *(mucositis)* are also potential side effects. Whether or not a certain symptom occurs depends both on the regimen and the patient. Your doctors and nurses are a good source of information on what to expect from whatever program is being recommended.

Most of the side effects from chemotherapy are short-term, and they go away after completion of the treatment. Permanent side effects can include early menopause (permanent shutdown of the ovaries), rare cases of congestive heart failure from the drug Adriamycin and the even rarer development of pre-leukemia (myelodysplasia) and leukemia years after treatment. See Chapter 9, Managing the Side Effects of Treatment.

HIGH-DOSE CHEMOTHERAPY/STEM CELL TRANSPLANTS: High-dose chemotherapy regimens using drug doses five to ten times stronger than standard chemotherapy treatments have been tested in breast cancer patients, with the hope of overcoming a tumor's drug resistance and achieving more cures. The dose-limiting toxicity of many chemotherapy drugs is the effect on the bone marrow stem cells—the cells that give rise to the white blood cells, red blood cells and platelets that circulate in our blood. High-dose regimens destroy the bone marrow. Therefore, high-dose chemotherapy approaches require collection and reinfusion of a patient's own bone marrow stem cells.

Early results of small trials of high-dose chemotherapy in breast cancer patients were promising, but results from many large, well-planned randomized clinical trials of high-dose chemotherapy versus standard-dose chemotherapy in both metastatic and earlier stage breast cancer failed to demonstrate any benefit of higher chemotherapy doses to patients. Additionally, high-dose therapy was quite toxic. High-dose chemotherapy for breast cancer should only be considered in the setting of a clinical trial.

Biologic Therapy

In recent years, researchers have been working to develop novel biologically targeted therapies for the treatment of cancer. These targeted therapies work differently from chemotherapy and are designed to look for certain markers on cancer cells or work on specific pathways important for cell growth.

TRASTUZUMAB (HERCEPTIN): The presence of the growth factor HER-2 on the surface of breast cancer cells is associated with a poorer outcome. In the tumors of up to 25 percent of breast cancer patients, the gene responsible for the production of HER-2 is increased from the usual two copies, in some cases up to over thirty copies (called gene amplification). The HER-2 status of a cancer can be determined by immunohistochemical (IHC) testing or fluorescence in situ hybridization (FISH) testing. When a cell has too many HER-2 receptors, the result is excessive growth of the cancer cells.

Herceptin is a drug used to treat breast cancer that overexpresses HER-2. It is a monoclonal antibody that works by binding to the HER-2 receptors on the surface of the cell and suppressing excess growth. Herceptin was approved in 1998 for the treatment of women with HER-2 positive metastatic breast cancer. It is given intravenously in an outpatient setting, most commonly once a week or every three weeks, either alone or in combination with certain chemotherapy agents. In 2005, four large, randomized clinical trials showed a substantial benefit for the addition of Herceptin to standard chemotherapy in early stage, HER-2-positive breast cancer patients.

Herceptin is generally well tolerated, with the main side effect being fever and chills, mostly associated with the first dose. Herceptin does not cause hair loss, low blood counts or nausea and vomiting. Heart problems, rarely symptomatic or life threatening, have been seen with this drug, particularly when given in combination with chemotherapy. Occasional evaluations of heart function are therefore recommended for patients receiving Herceptin.

BEVACIZUMAB (AVASTIN): Avastin is a monoclonal antibody that binds to an important protein called vascular endothelial growth factor (VEGF). VEGF is responsible for new blood vessel growth in normal cells as well as in cancerous tumors. Avastin works by blocking the growth of these new blood vessels, which carry food and oxygen to the tumor, essentially choking the blood supply to the tumor and causing it to die. By doing this, Avastin helps chemotherapy drugs kill more cancer cells.

Avastin, which is approved for treating advanced colorectal cancer and has proven efficacy in lung cancer, may also have a role in the treatment of breast cancer. A recent clinical trial showed that adding Avastin to the chemotherapy drug Taxol nearly doubled the time it took for cancer to grow in women with metastatic breast cancer, compared with women who received Taxol alone. Many additional clinical trials of Avastin in both early stage and metastatic breast cancer are ongoing.

Overall, Avastin is very well tolerated with minimal side effects. These include high blood pressure and a small increased risk of blood clots.

Bisphosphonates

Bisphosphonates are a class of drugs most commonly used to prevent and treat osteoporosis, since their main action is to prevent bone breakdown. Recent studies have shown that bisphosphonates added to chemotherapy or endocrine therapy can reduce pain, fractures and other complications of bone metastases due to breast cancer.

Pamidronate (Aredia) and zoledronic acid (Zometa) are the bisphosphonates available in the United States for the treatment of bone metastases. Both are given by intravenous infusion every three to four weeks. Ibandronate (Bondronat, Boniva) and clodronate (Bonefos) are bisphosphonates available in oral form that are approved in other parts of the world. An ongoing clinical trial (SWOG S0307) is comparing several of these bisphosphonates in the early stage breast cancer setting, with the hope of preventing bone metastases from occurring.

Intravenous Access/Implantable Venous Access Devices

Chemotherapy drugs can be introduced into the body in a number of ways, but most drugs are given *intravenously* (by vein). If the treatment is given by a needle into an arm (peripheral) vein, there are measures to take to make this a safe procedure. First, in the case of breast surgery that involves lymph node dissection, it is important not to use the affected arm for intravenous infusion of chemotherapy drugs. The changes in circulation put a patient at a higher risk of infections and lymphedema in that arm. With some chemotherapy drugs it is also important not to have blood drawn from the same arm that the nurses will use for chemotherapy. Finally, to make veins easier to find, use heat (such as a warm blanket or warm water from the faucet) and drink plenty of fluids. Heat helps veins expand, and drinking a lot of fluids will make the veins "plump," in both cases making veins easier to find.

Implantable Venous Access Devices

ಌ

- Implantable Ports (Portacaths): The port is a small disc about 1½ inches in diameter. It has a raised center or septum, which is made from a self-sealing rubber material. The septum is where the needle is inserted for delivery of medication or for blood draws. The medication is carried from the port into the bloodstream through a small, flexible tube called a catheter. The port is inserted under the skin below the collarbone. Implantable ports can also be placed under the skin of the arm, above the elbow. Portacaths require a heparin (anticlotting) flush every three to four weeks to keep the line flowing. They cause minimal alteration in appearance because they are totally under the skin, and there is no disruption to showering or bathing.

- External Sialastic Catheters (Hickmans®, Broviacs®, Groshongs®): An external catheter is a hollow tube made of rubber that is inserted into the large vein leading to the heart. The end of the catheter looks like an IV line in your chest. Blood draws and medication administration can be done directly from the end of the external catheter, avoiding needle sticks. The external catheters have a slightly higher rate of infections. These catheters require more home care, including daily heparin flushes and dressing changes. There is more of an alteration in body image and physical freedom with this type of catheter because of the four to five inches of tubing extending from the chest wall. Care must be taken when showering, bathing and swimming.

For patients who are facing frequent chemotherapy treatments or longer infusions of chemotherapy, those who have hard to find or collapsible veins or those who have a personal preference, there are catheters or shunts that can be surgically placed and remain in the patient for weeks or months. There are pros and cons to implantable venous catheters. The catheter eliminates the need to put needles into the arm for blood draws and chemotherapy. Placement of the catheter requires a surgery, although it is a minor outpatient procedure. If a definite recommendation of chemotherapy is made prior to the final breast surgery, the catheter device can be placed at the same time, eliminating the need for one more procedure. Placement of the catheter should be carefully determined to avoid irritation from clothing (like bra straps) rubbing on the site. Catheter complications can include infection, clots, or, rarely, a lung being punctured (pneumothorax) during the placement of the catheter. In general, they are very safe.

All types of implantable venous access devices can be used to draw blood, infuse drugs and transfuse blood. Your specific therapy may influence which type of device is best for you. Check with your medical team.

I was diagnosed with breast cancer in February. My treatment lasted 10 months and included surgery, chemotherapy and radiation. Because of my cancer experience, I changed careers and now work in cancer patient education and outreach. For me, cancer had a silver lining which has allowed me to do new things. I painted the top of my bald head with the basketball numbers of my oldest granddaughter. At her game during half time, I stood up, took off my hat, and bowed my head towards my granddaughter. I received a standing ovation!

This photo was taken about two months after I completed treatment. Here we are in all of our glory, the three bald ones!

—Janet Parker, diagnosed in 1997 at age 54

CHAPTER 9

ॐ

Managing the Side Effects of Treatment

Fatigue

Fatigue is the most commonly reported side effect of chemotherapy. It is the feeling of being tired not only physically but emotionally as well. It means having less energy to do the things you are used to doing.

The most commonly asked question is, "Can I still work?" If possible, taking the first few weeks off from work will allow you to focus on you for the time being and then later decide if work is something you are up for. Most people can arrange with their employers to take time off, decrease to part time or obtain the flexibility to take frequent breaks at work. Some people may take the first few weeks off and assess how they actually feel after receiving a few doses. Your health care provider will likely support you in obtaining disability insurance if you need to take time off from work.

There is no wrong decision regarding how much you work or accomplish while receiving chemotherapy, and remember that your fatigue will resolve after your treatments are completed. The best advice is to listen to your body, rest when needed and ask for help from your friends and family.

Hair Loss (Alopecia)

Some, but not all, chemotherapies cause hair loss. A commonly used drug, doxorubicin (Adriamycin), will cause total body hair loss within two to three weeks of the first dose in most patients. Some people may choose to cut their hair short or have a friend or family member shave it off once hair loss starts. Some find it helpful to meet with a cranial prosthesis specialist, also known as a wig specialist, prior to losing their hair so they can try to create the same look and obtain a good fit. Most insurance companies will cover this service with a prescription. Alternatively, wearing a wig may not be for you. Some prefer to wear nothing and others prefer a head covering; this is an individual choice. Your hair will grow back after chemotherapy is completed. For those who are receiving chemotherapy that may cause only minimal hair loss, perms and dyes will likely prevent hair loss from becoming significantly noticeable.

Mucositis

Mucositis involves mouth ulcerations or mouth sores that are caused by chemotherapy. This affects 30 to 40 percent of people receiving chemotherapy. The reason for mucositis is that the oral environment is not balanced. The symptoms of mucositis are varying sizes of sores in the mouth, inability to eat certain foods that are hot or spicy and mouth pain. You may have a decreased nutritional intake as a result. Treatment varies based on the severity, and your chemotherapy may be reduced in dosage if the mucositis is severe enough. Good oral hygiene-including brushing, flossing and salt water gargles-will help to prevent mucositis.

Neutropenia

Low white blood counts *(neutropenia)* are one of the more serious side effects of chemotherapy, but the risk depends on the kind of chemotherapy or treatment protocol. The kind of white blood cell that fights infection is called a neutrophil. If your neutrophils are too low there is an increased risk for infection. During your treatment your neutrophil counts will be monitored to make sure you are safe for the next treatment dose. It is possible that you may need to start a growth factor, such as filgrastim (Neupogen) or pegfilgrastim (Neulasta), that is given as a subcutaneous injection. These growth factors are commonly used when needed to keep your neutrophil counts at a safe level until your treatment is complete.

Nausea

Not all chemotherapies carry the same side effects, and nausea can vary from mild to moderate to severe. There are a variety of anti-nausea medications to help with this. For years more simple regimens such as prochloraperazine (Compazine) and lorazepam (Ativan) have been used. New agents are in a separate class called serotonin receptor antagonists and include Zofran, Kytril and Aloxi. A new drug used in cases of severe nausea is aprepitant (Emend).

Some of these medications are used by themselves and some work better when given in combination with other anti-nausea drugs. Communicate your symptoms to your caregiver team and ask for recommendations on how to use these medications in a way that will suit your needs. Alternative options such as nutritional supplements and acupuncture help some patients. While receiving chemotherapy, maintaining a well-balanced diet with small, frequent meals will also help combat nausea.

Menstrual Changes

If you are premenopausal you are likely to have amenorrhea, the absence of menses, which could be temporary or permanent depending on your age. Possible side effects associated with menopause include hot flashes and vaginal dryness. See Chapter 18, Menopause without Hormones.

Supplements

Many people ask if it is okay to take supplements such as herbs and vitamins during chemotherapy. Discuss this with your physician. Generally, taking a simple multivitamin and eating a healthy diet is the safest thing to do.

Prostheses and Bras

One of the issues after breast cancer surgery is selecting an appropriate *prosthesis*. Mastectomy patients generally are instructed not to wear a bra for several weeks after surgery, until their incision has adequately healed and swelling has subsided. After surgery, wearing a postoperative garment-such as a camisole or leisure bra-is recommended while you are working or at social functions or if you are usually more comfortable in a supportive undergarment. Your physician will be able to determine when you are physically ready to proceed with a consultation at a prosthesis retailer.

CAMISOLES: A cotton camisole should fit snugly against the body with no inside seams to irritate incisions. The sizes range from XS to XXL and accommodate a variety of body types; the wearer adds fiberfill into pockets as needed to achieve a normal shape. There are also versions that have detachable pouches for drainage management immediately after surgery, for use with Jackson-Pratt, Hemovac and other drainage systems.

Prices on postoperative camisoles vary depending on the manufacturer and are available where breast prostheses are sold. Camisoles may be reimbursed by your insurance provider, but usually require a physician's prescription. In the case of Medicare reimbursement, the prescription must be dated *after* the date of surgery. Some hospitals routinely provide these items in their postsurgery care.

LEISURE BRAS: Longer elastic banding under the bustline area and cotton fabric make leisure bras a comfortable choice to transition into a more traditional style bra. Front hooks allow easy access for dressing without straining the underarm area. This type of garment can be a good choice during radiation. Contour shaping can be added with a foam or prosthesis form or fiberfill stuffing. Sizing is generalized: 34 to 46 A/B or C/D.

PROSTHESES: Not every woman who has a mastectomy chooses to wear a breast prosthesis or breast form. The decision is a matter of choice. A breast prosthesis may assist women in adapting to changes in body appearance and weight distribution after a mastectomy.

Prostheses are made from silicone, foam or fiberfill. Some fit into a bra with or without special pockets to hold them in place. There are also several prosthesis options that attach to the body. One system involves adhesive strips that apply to the chest wall, and the breast form attaches with a Velcro inset. Another choice is a breast prosthesis with a silicone gel strip that enables it to attach directly to the chest wall without strips. Many women enjoy the freedom of movement that an attachable form introduces, since the weight is on the front of the body instead of on the shoulder area.

Prostheses come in various shapes, sizes and colors to accommodate different body types, breast shapes, surgeries and personal preferences. Getting a good fit is important, and it may require fortitude and patience. Some women find it helpful to take along an experienced friend (or an American Cancer Society Reach to Recovery volunteer, see Appendix B, Organization and Resources). Finding an experienced retailer is also important. The prosthesis should match the remaining breast in order to maintain body weight equilibrium and prevent back, neck and posture problems. The current trend is toward lighter-weight silicone breast forms. This can be an ideal selection for women with osteoporosis, arthritis or lymphedema. However, women who are active and mobile should wear a form that is weighted enough to keep the bra anchored and the breast weight equalized. A certified fitter will be able to assist with appropriate selection. Also communicate to your fit consultant your lifestyle activities so she can help you select a form that is appropriate for you. Schedule at least one hour for your initial fitting appointment so you have enough time to make a comfortable decision without being rushed. Many women also investigate prosthesis options prior to surgery so they can make educated choices about their options after surgery.

BRA FIT: Many surgeries involve only partial breast removal or lumpectomies and breast-conserving methods. There are a number of options available to help with symmetry after these types of surgery. Check with a certified fitter to investigate preferred bra styles that equalize the size and shape of breasts, or partial silicone shells that add slight contouring but not the weight of a full form.

After breast surgery it is important to be fitted for a comfortable and supportive bra. Make sure the bra fits and supports you, hugging the chest wall and the underside of the arm and cup area. No flesh should overflow the top or underarm area. If you have an existing breast, make sure the bra fit contains the full breast capacity so the prosthesis form can be sized appropriately for the other side. The bottom of the bra should fit so that it anchors down comfortably snug and low on the small of the back (not over the shoulder blades). The front of the band should fit flush against the chest wall so the center tacks and there is no gaping or bowing at the top. Straps should not cut into the shoulder, since the bra should be supporting from under the bustline not pulling from the top. For bra fit after a bilateral mastectomy, try a style with a fuller band on the bottom to help anchor the bra down, and with fuller coverage on the top edge so the forms do not fall away from the body when you bend over.

PRICE AND INSURANCE: Many retailers will modify bras for use with prostheses free of charge or for a nominal fee, so if you have a bra that fit well prior to surgery, bring it with you to the fitting appointment.

Prosthesis products vary in price according to the quality, warranty and comfort. Most insurance providers will cover the cost of breast prostheses and mastectomy bras, especially if the physician writes a prescription with medical necessity documentation. It is important to verify individual eligibility and coverage with your insurance group before purchasing these products. It is also wise to bring to your fitting a prescription or referral for all items that you are seeking insurance coverage for. Medicare does cover a percentage of the cost of these products, but the prescription should be dated before the date of purchase. Many retailers are familiar with insurance requirements and may be able to help facilitate the process.

Women without insurance have options as well. Contact the local American Cancer Society patient services or Y-ME for assistance with securing a prosthesis free of charge or for a nominal fee.

From *My Garden*, a "nipple painting" that became an art print to raise funding for non-profit agencies. For more information, visit www. laposart.com.

—*Freeda Lapos Babson, Breast Cancer Survivor*

CHAPTER 10

🍠

Young Women and
Breast Cancer

Young women can and do get breast cancer even in their 30s and sometimes younger. In 2006 in the United States alone, about 10,000 young
women under the age of 40 will be told that they have breast cancer. Of
these, about 1,000 will be between 20 and 30 years old. Over 250,000 women
under the age of 40 are living with breast cancer. The good news is that survival rates are increasing every day with new treatments and therapies.

Because breast cancer is not considered common in women under age 40,
having the disease can be a very isolating experience for a younger woman.
Young women with breast cancer have special issues that are often not
addressed by the medical community, including issues with delayed diagnosis and medical treatment, fertility, sexuality, genetic risk and future risk.
There are also unique social issues involving balancing motherhood, career
and relationships. Talking to your children about your cancer can be very
difficult. Appendix C, Publications, lists many books and pamphlets that
can help with this, or visit the American Cancer Society website at www.
cancer.org.

Diagnosis

Diagnosing breast cancer is often more difficult in younger women because
their breast tissue is more dense than breast tissue in older women, and there
is a general bias that women under age 40 do not get breast cancer. Since
women under 40 typically do not have mammograms, it is even more criti-
cal that they do breast self-exams on a regular basis. Do not ignore warning

signs, such as lumps or unusual discharge. Young women must be assertive and not accept the line "you are too young to get breast cancer." See your health care provider if you have symptoms, and get a second opinion if your health care provider adopts a "wait and see" approach.

Treatment

Early detection and treatment significantly improve a woman's chance of survival. The course of breast cancer treatment at any age is based on the stage of the disease, as well as the woman's health and personal circumstances.

Contraception

If you are sexually active it is important to discuss contraception with your health care team. It is generally recommended that women going through treatment for breast cancer use nonhormonal methods of contraception.

Fertility Issues

For many young women, having children is an important part of moving forward with a life after cancer. Breast cancer treatments may affect your ability to have children; however, parenthood options are available to you. Talk to your oncologist before you start treatment.

Surgery and radiation for breast cancer do not usually affect your reproductive system or fertility, but they can affect your ability to breastfeed. However, chemotherapy can increase your risk of early menopause.

About half of the women under age 40 who have chemotherapy may stop having periods during treatment. Sometimes, menses will start again after treatment ends. All women who have chemotherapy are at risk for early menopause because chemotherapy reduces your egg supply. Talk to your doctor about your risks.

There are a number of parenthood options for you before, during and after breast cancer treatment. Talk to your heath care provider about these options. Fertile Hope (www.fertilehope.org) offers fertility information for young women faced with cancer treatment.

Relationships

Breast cancer in younger women can affect self-esteem, sexuality and relationships. Most of the side effects are temporary, but depression is very common during and after treatment, so young women should be encouraged to talk to their doctors. During treatment, many women benefit from a supportive environment that involves peer support from other young breast cancer patients and survivors, family and friends and counseling. Life will never be the same, but with the support of friends and family, it can be very rewarding. The Young Survival Coalition (www.youngsurvival.org) provides information and support to young women with breast cancer.

Employment

Managing job responsibilities while in treatment can be challenging. Although many women with breast cancer do work through the entire treatment cycle, they often do so at a reduced level. Companies with fifty or more employees are obligated by law to provide twelve weeks of unpaid medical leave. Often, women need more time than this due to longer treatment periods. Employers may accommodate an employee's needs by creating a modified work schedule. Some employers allow employees to donate their sick time to assist fellow employees during an illness. Contact your company's benefits coordinator and learn about the options your employer may offer.

I was diagnosed with breast cancer in the springtime. I noticed one of my nipples looked different—it was retracted. When I felt around it, I found the lump. I hadn't been doing self-exams. I was young and had no family history. This picture was taken at Thanksgiving, and I had just completed 25 of 27 weekly chemotherapy treatments. My surgery and six weeks of radiation are scheduled to start after the holidays. By spring I hope to feel well enough to go running with my dog Emily.

—Katherine Ellis, diagnosed in 2005 at age 31

꙳

Chapter 11

Clinical Trials

Advances in medicine and science are the direct result of new ideas and approaches developed through careful research. In the field of medicine, research studies conducted with patients are called *clinical trials*. A clinical trial is an organized study that tries to answer specific scientific questions and to find new and better ways to prevent, diagnose and treat diseases. Participation in clinical trials could potentially benefit many people by providing treatments beyond those that currently exist and by increasing knowledge about a disease and its potential treatments. Clinical trials are an extremely important way to evaluate new approaches to diseases such as cancer and are a scientific way to test new agents or procedures while ensuring safety.

Types of Clinical Trials

There are many kinds of clinical trials. They range from studies of ways to prevent, detect, diagnose, control and treat cancer to studies of the disease's psychological impact and ways to improve the patient's quality of life and comfort. In cancer research, a clinical trial generally refers to the evaluation of treatment methods such as a new drug, surgery or imaging technology or a new way of using known standard drugs and treatments. Cancer clinical trials that deal with new approaches to treatment most often involve the use of surgery, radiation therapy, endocrine therapy, chemotherapy or biologic therapy. Depending on what is being studied, a particular trial may involve patients with cancer or people who do not have cancer but who are at a higher risk than most people for developing it. Many of today's most effective interventions are the direct result of knowledge gained through clinical trials.

The search for good cancer treatments often begins with basic research in the laboratory and in animal studies before new therapies are tested in patients. Based on what researchers learn from laboratory studies, as well as from previous clinical studies, new therapies are designed to take advantage of what has worked in the past and to improve upon these techniques.

Trial Specifics

STUDY PROTOCOL: A *protocol* is a carefully constructed treatment plan investigating an experimental procedure or treatment. Most protocols are developed by a group of scientists, researchers and doctors. Protocols are written to define a treatment plan that meets or exceeds the accepted standard of care for a certain disease. Research protocols are designed to answer research questions and to protect the patient. The protocol explains what the trial will do, how and why. An investigator—an experienced clinical researcher—uses the protocol in the treatment of patients.

PARTICIPATION: In order to most accurately evaluate the effectiveness of a treatment, clinical trials must be carefully managed and follow strict scientific guidelines. Specific characteristics make up the eligibility criteria, which are used to identify people who can participate in a certain trial. In most cancer treatment trials, results will only be reliable if everyone has specified, similar aspects of their disease. Some other common eligibility requirements include age, general health, the stage and extent of disease, previous treatments and the type of cancer. These criteria also help to ensure the safety of participants by protecting them from known risks.

STUDY CONDUCT: In the United States, clinical trials may be conducted or overseen by a clinical trials cooperative group (an organized group of oncologists from a number of hospitals and clinics), an institution (a qualified oncologist or group of oncologists in an institution or clinic) or a pharmaceutical or biotechnology company. Most clinical trials are conducted at major academic medical centers, but patients can also receive treatment at a local medical center or physician's office, depending on the type of trial. Community hospitals and doctors are becoming a significant part of the research network. Community Clinical Oncology Programs (CCOPs) link community physicians with *National Cancer Institute* (NCI) clinical research programs, so that more cancer patients can participate in clinical trials in their own communities.

Major cooperative groups involved in breast cancer clinical trials that are supported by the NCI include the National Surgical Adjuvant Breast and Bowel Project (NSABP), the Southwest Oncology Group (SWOG), the Cancer and Leukemia Group B (CALGB), the Eastern Cooperative Oncology Group (ECOG) and the North Central Cancer Treatment Group (NCCTG).

Phases of Clinical Trials

Clinical trials are conducted in steps called phases, each designed to find out certain information. Patients may be eligible for studies in different phases, depending on a patient's general condition and the type and stage of cancer. Each new phase of a clinical trial depends on and builds on information from an earlier phase.

PHASE I: Phase I cancer studies determine the safety of a new treatment. In a Phase I study, a new research treatment is given to a small number of patients. These treatments have been tested in laboratory and animal studies but not in humans. Phase I studies of new drugs determine how best to give the drug (orally, intravenously, etc.), how often and how much can be given safely. Although the research treatment has been well tested in laboratory and animal studies, the side effects in patients cannot be completely known ahead of time. Since Phase I studies may involve significant risks and are of unproven benefit, they are generally not offered to patients who have other, proven treatment options available to them. Phase I studies may produce anticancer effects, and some patients have been helped by these treatments.

These studies often involve dose escalation, by starting with a low dose not expected to cause serious toxicity in any patients, and then increasing the dose for subsequent patients according to a preplanned series of steps. The dose can be increased by giving more at one time or by giving the same dose more often. Once the best dose is chosen, the drug is studied for its ability to shrink tumors in Phase II trials.

PHASE II: Phase II cancer studies determine the effect of a research treatment on cancer. They are designed to find out if the treatment is effective in fighting cancer in humans and also to generate more information about safety and risks. Phase II studies are conducted with larger numbers of patients and usually focus on a particular type of cancer.

PHASE III: Phase III cancer studies are designed to determine whether a new treatment is more effective and/or less toxic than a standard therapy (the treatment most accepted). If a treatment shows activity against cancer in a Phase II study, it moves on to Phase III. In Phase III studies, the new treatment is directly compared to the standard one to see which is more effective.

Large cooperative group studies are important in Phase III studies because they typically involve many patients in determining whether two treatments are actually different or whether differences could be due to chance. Statistical results are influenced greatly by the number of patients treated in the study, with larger studies having a greater likelihood of obtaining a definitive answer about treatment differences.

Patient Protection

One way to prevent patient or doctor bias from influencing study results is randomization. A randomized clinical trial is a Phase III study in which patients with similar traits (such as extent of disease) are assigned by chance to one of the treatments being studied—either the new intervention or the standard intervention. Because irrelevant factors or preferences do not influence the distribution of patients, the treatment groups can be considered comparable and results of the different treatments used in different groups can be compared.

The group that receives standard treatment is called the *control arm* and receives what experts view as the best treatment available. The group receiving the experimental therapy is called the experimental arm and receives a treatment that experts think may have equal benefit or advantages over the standard treatment. Sometimes no standard treatment exists for certain groups of patients. In such cases, one group of patients might receive the new drug and the other group none. No patient is placed in a control group without treatment if there is any known treatment that would benefit the patient. Patients in the control group are monitored as often and as carefully as those in the treatment group.

A double-blind study is one in which neither the patient nor the physician knows which drug (or dose) the patient is getting. In single-blind studies, patients do not know which of several treatments they are receiving (to prevent personal bias from influencing a patient's reactions and study results), but the medical team does. In such blinded studies, the treatment can be quickly identified, if necessary, by a special code.

To further prevent patient or medical team bias from influencing study results, placebos and other blinding procedures are sometimes used. A *placebo* is an inactive substance resembling a medication and is used as a control to compare a medicine believed to be active. It is usually a tablet, capsule or injection that contains a harmless substance but in appearance is the same as the medicine being tested. A placebo may be compared with a new drug when no one knows whether any drug or treatment will be effective.

An investigational new drug (IND) is a drug allowed by the Food and Drug Administration (FDA) to be used in clinical trials but that is not approved for commercial marketing or general use. New cancer treatments must prove to be safe and effective in scientific studies before they can be made widely available. *Phase IV* is a term sometimes used to describe the continuing evaluation of a new drug because it is used after FDA approval and in combination with other treatments.

With any new treatment, there may be risks as well as possible benefits. Today, clinical trials are regulated by a number of governing groups and processes to ensure patient safety, comfort and benefit from scientific research. Patients' well-being during clinical trials is most notably protected by the informed consent process, peer review and an Institutional Review Board (IRB) that scrutinizes all research involving humans.

The process in which a patient learns about the purpose and protocol of a clinical trial and agrees to participate is called *informed consent*. Anyone entering a clinical trial is required to sign a form indicating that she understands what will and may happen during the study. It is crucial that an individual receive and clearly understand as much information as possible before agreeing to participate in a clinical trial. Patients must be aware of the treatment to be given, medical procedures, side effects and the possible risks and benefits. Patients should decide whether they want to take part in a study only after they understand both the possible risks and the benefits. The informed consent also indicates which costs are covered by the study and states clearly that patients have the right to leave the study at any time without giving up access to other treatments. This decision, along with any questions concerning the study, should always be discussed between the patient and her health care team.

Insurance Coverage

Although clinical studies are an integral part of cancer treatment, some insurance policies do not reimburse patients' costs for clinical trials or experimental drugs. Fortunately, the majority of insurance companies recognize that patients enrolled in cancer clinical trials would require therapy whether or not they are in a trial and do cover most of the medical costs for such patients.

In trials involving investigational new drugs, patients are sometimes provided with free drugs or procedures, although they (or their insurer) are charged for clinic costs. Cancer center financial counselors and clinical research study coordinators should be able to help patients determine and obtain insurance coverage for a given study. A doctor's letter that outlines the study protocol and documents the patient's eligibility for the trial may sometimes be necessary to obtain insurance company approval for a clinical trial.

Patient Participation

Patients take part in clinical trials for many reasons. Usually, they hope they will benefit from participation: a cure of disease, a longer time to live or a way to feel better. Often they want to contribute to a research effort that may help others. Knowledge gained from clinical trials has been, and continues to be, essential to advancing the understanding of breast cancer. Major scientific discoveries in the laboratory are leading to exciting new approaches against breast cancer (see Chapter 20, Breast Cancer Research: Hope for the Future). The goal is to translate the best of that research into findings that directly help patients. Clinical trials, the link between basic research and patient care, offer hope for the future.

When I was diagnosed I wanted to talk with other Black women, but the Black women in my church and social groups felt that breast cancer was very private and they wanted to keep it a secret. God has asked me to speak out and reach other senior Black women of the "Dinosaur Age" and tell them about getting mammograms, doing breast self exams and the importance of finding breast cancer early. After my surgery, I found a great survivor and support group and attending their monthly meetings has given me inspiration.

— Evalena Hatcher, diagnosed in 2002 at age 68

❧

Chapter 12

Incorporating Complementary Therapies into the Treatment Program

Complementary and alternative medicine (CAM) therapies are those treatments and strategies that are not commonly available from, but may be used in addition to, "conventional" medicine. They include nutritional supplements, botanicals (herbs), diets, lifestyle changes, massage, manipulation of joints (including chiropractic), exercise, mind-body strategies (including visualization, guided imagery, meditation and hypnosis), acupuncture, oriental medicine and more. Some of these treatments have been shown to offer benefits such as cancer preventive activity, support of *immune system* function, improved quality of life and solutions to some specific health issues. Although CAM therapies can provide significant benefits, they are not a substitute for conventional cancer treatments such as chemotherapy, radiation, surgery and biologic therapies. Conventional cancer treatments provide interventions that are not available from CAM therapies.

While many CAM therapies are relatively noninvasive, gentle and from natural sources, they still have the potential to interfere with conventional treatment, worsening adverse effects and causing some cancers to progress more quickly.

There are many popular CAM therapies and products available with an equal number of health claims. The most common of these are described briefly below. In order to enjoy the maximum benefit from such treatments, use only licensed providers with experience in treating cancer survivors. In addition, be certain that your conventional providers know what other therapies and products you are using.

Types of Complementary Therapies

DIET AND NUTRITION: Diet and nutrition can play a positive role in cancer prevention, helping maintain your general health, and can have a positive effect during conventional treatment. Many diet and nutritional supplements are reasonable and effective, while others are extreme and can worsen your status. If you plan to revise your diet and improve your nutrition, enlist the support of a licensed health care provider. See also Chapter 13, Using Nutrition in the Fight Against Breast Cancer.

ACUPUNCTURE AND ORIENTAL MEDICINE: Needles and Chinese herbs, also known as traditional Chinese medicine (TCM), are used in a system of diagnosis with logic and have applications that often differ significantly from Western thinking. Acupuncture and Oriental medicine have been used to treat many different human diseases in Asia for centuries. Acupuncture has been shown to be useful in controlling nausea and vomiting as well as some painful conditions. Chinese herbs are subject to the same comments as botanical medicines, below.

BOTANICAL (HERBAL) MEDICINES: Botanicals offer a wide variety of treatment actions. Many modern drugs are based on herbs. Some of the herbs that are available over the counter have actions in your body as powerful as some prescription drugs. Botanicals can, in some cases, provide safe, effective treatment for a wide range of ailments. They can also, however, interact with drugs or other conventional treatments and may have side effects that are not explained on the label. The appropriate use of botanical medicines can be as complex as conventional drugs. The best results are usually achieved with the guidance of a licensed expert.

HOMEOPATHY: Homeopathy is a unique treatment method that uses very dilute mixtures of herbs, minerals and other substances to treat a wide variety of symptoms. Homeopathics are widely used and accepted in some European and other countries but are still considered controversial in the United States and should be considered with the same comments and cautions as botanical medicines, above.

MASSAGE THERAPY: Massage therapy has been well received by many cancer survivors. A variety of massage techniques are available. A few simple precautions and checking in with your physician will give you a safe, rewarding entry to this comforting therapy with a licensed massage practitioner.

MUSIC THERAPY: Music therapy can provide benefits of relaxation, stress relief and a comforting diversion.

COUNSELING: Counseling can provide relaxation, stress relief and added perspective, especially when dealing with cancer. In some cases, counseling can help improve your coping skills and provide some peace of mind with just a few visits. It is important to find a counselor whose interests, experience, personality and perspective mesh well with yours.

MANIPULATION: Manipulation of the spine and extremities can sometimes provide pain relief and improved function. There are significant variations in the services available from different licensed providers. Forceful applications of manipulation may not be advisable for cancer survivors. Find a provider who shares your objectives. Check with your physicians to be certain that no exceptional circumstances should be considered.

PHYSICAL THERAPEUTICS (INCLUDING EXERCISE): Physical therapeutics can reduce pain, improve function for a wide variety of complaints and can help prepare patients to return to their activities of daily living. Exercise also has a disease prevention component.

Sources for Complementary Therapies

There are a number of sources for CAM treatment, including naturopathic physicians, acupuncturists, massage therapists, chiropractors, physical therapists, counselors and more. Some have specific training and knowledge in dealing with the special considerations of cancer survivors. The most commonly utilized provider types are described below.

NATUROPATHIC PHYSICIANS: In Washington State, naturopathic physicians are licensed primary care providers who use clinical nutrition, botanical medicine (herbs), some Chinese medicines, manipulation, counseling, massage, some physical therapeutics and other natural therapies. In addition, naturopathic physicians can write prescriptions for certain drugs and can perform some office surgery procedures. Most specialize in certain areas and some offer additional services such as hydrotherapy, acupuncture and natural childbirth.

Naturopathic physicians strongly support the body's innate ability to heal itself but also cooperate with conventional medical interventions. Naturopathic physicians use the designation ND, which is not the same as MD.

ACUPUNCTURISTS AND ORIENTAL MEDICINE: In Washington State, acupuncturists are licensed by the Washington State Department of Health. They practice TCM, which can include acupuncture, traditional Chinese herbs, heat therapy (moxibustion), massage, exercise and dietary advice. The objective of Chinese medicine is to help the body heal.

TCM is considered by some to be a type of energy medicine, focusing on and treating the body's energy in "meridians" that traverse the body. Licensed acupuncturists utilize the designation LAC.

LICENSED MASSAGE PRACTITIONERS: In Washington State, massage practitioners are licensed. Massage therapy can provide important relaxation and other benefits for cancer survivors. Many massage therapists do not treat cancer survivors because of concerns about harming the patient, but this modality can be used safely and effectively when coordinated with your primary health care provider.

COUNSELORS: Licensed counselors can provide a variety of services, including stress counseling, imagery, visualization and other mind-body strategies.

OTHER SOURCES: Some CAM providers are not licensed or regulated by the State of Washington. These include music therapists, some exercise trainers and others. If you are pursuing such a therapy, it is usually best to find a referral from someone you trust, such as an existing provider. Other support organizations such as Cancer Lifeline, Gilda's Club and the American Cancer Society can also provide helpful information. See Appendix B, Organizations and Resources.

Getting the Best Result

Many unregulated sources of information about CAM exist on the Internet, in advertising, from salespersons and in the media. Some of this information is accurate and some is not.

In Washington State, licensure is required of some but not all providers. Licensure provides a degree of assurance that providers have met minimum training, experience, competence and background requirements. Such protections do not exist with unlicensed persons. "Certifications" by organizations that are not government-regulated may not be meaningful. Letters after a person's name may not have any meaning when it comes to providing safe and effective services for cancer survivors.

- Use services from providers licensed by the Washington State Department of Health. Unlicensed providers may have minimal or no training.

- Insist that your medical specialists know about all treatments you are pursuing.

- Require that all treatment-specific providers, such as naturopathic physicians, acupuncturists, and so on, provide your medical specialists with written reports of what they are doing.

- Ask for referrals. Medical specialists and staff are often a good source for finding CAM providers who understand the special needs of cancer survivors.

I was diagnosed with breast cancer on my birthday. I felt completely isolated. Since then, however, I have been involved in a support and networking group for young women. It has been the most important part of learning to live as a young breast cancer survivor and not feel alone.

—Polly Halpern, diagnosed in 2002 at age 35

❧

Chapter 13

Using Nutrition
in the Fight
Against Breast Cancer

More and more research points to the effect of diet and exercise on health. Poor diet, obesity and lack of regular exercise can increase the risk of developing breast and other types of cancer, heart disease and diabetes. Diet factors associated with increased risk of breast cancer include excessive calorie intake (resulting in being overweight or obese) and drinking alcohol. After being diagnosed with breast cancer, you can make diet and lifestyle changes to reduce the risk of breast cancer recurrence and to improve your overall health and quality of life.

Obesity and being overweight have been associated with poorer breast cancer outcome. Weight gain during breast cancer treatment may increase the risk of breast cancer recurrence. During and after breast cancer treatment, work to maintain a healthy weight or to lose weight gradually through proper diet and physical activity.

Evidence shows that persons who consume a more plant-based diet have decreased risk of several chronic diseases, including heart disease, diabetes, some types of cancer and obesity.

NUTRITION TIPS:

- Eat a mostly plant-based diet, including a rainbow of vegetables and fruits, whole grains and plant proteins (such as legumes, including all types of beans, peas, lentils, nuts and nut butters).

- Limit fat intake and choose healthy fats (olive and canola oils, nuts, avocado and fish oils). Minimize saturated and partially hydrogenated fats.

- Consume sources of calcium and vitamin D for bone health (a dietitian can give you guidelines).
- Avoid alcohol. Use moderation if you drink.
- Consume only moderate amounts of soy and flax foods. It is currently unclear if persons with estrogen-positive breast cancer should consume or avoid soy foods, flaxseed or flax oil. These foods contain phytoestrogens ("plant estrogens," including isoflavones). Until more is known about the effects of phytoestrogens and isoflavones on breast cancer, it is recommended that breast cancer patients not exceed moderate intake of soy and flax in their diet and that they avoid excessive phytoestrogen/isoflavone supplements.

DIET GUIDELINES DURING CANCER TREATMENT:

- Drink eight to twelve cups of fluids daily, depending on your body size (water, juice, milk, soup or other liquids).
- Consume a protein-rich diet: legumes (including beans, peas, lentils, nuts and soy foods in moderation), milk, yogurt, eggs, fish, poultry and meat. Consider using whey, egg whites or soy protein powders if your intake of protein-rich foods is limited.
- Review your dietary supplements (vitamin, minerals, herbs, etc.) with your physician, pharmacist and dietician. Discuss if supplements may be continued during surgery, chemotherapy or radiation.
- Maintain activity to promote digestion, maintain strength and reduce risk of osteoporosis.
- Request an appointment with the registered dietician at your cancer care facility.

In the United States today, there are more than

two million breast cancer survivors.

❧

Chapter 14

Physical Rehabilitation

Exercise

Energy levels during cancer treatment and recovery after surgery will be different for every person, depending on the extent of the disease, the treatment received and other factors. Exercise presurgery can be beneficial for preventing and maintaining post-treatment fatigue. Exercises to regain motion and strength in the arms and shoulders can resume slowly and gently after surgery. Exercise is encouraged during radiation therapy and chemotherapy.

Regular exercise will help combat fatigue, enhance well-being, assist with weight control and decrease breast cancer risk. Recent studies indicate that three to four hours a week of moderate to vigorous levels of regular physical activity can reduce a woman's risk of developing breast cancer by up to 30 to 40 percent.

Ask your physician for a referral to the physical therapy program at your clinic or hospital. A lymphedema-trained physical therapist will teach you cardiovascular, arm strengthening and flexibility exercises to promote a return to your prior level of activity.

YOGA: Yoga can be beneficial physically, mentally and spiritually. Check your local Yellow Pages, or ask others who practice yoga about various centers. Look for a practitioner who has breast cancer knowledge.

QI GONG: Qi Gong is an active and intrinsic physical exercise that regulates the mind, breath and body. Regular practice can build your mental consciousness, strengthen internal functions and bring body and mind into balance.

Qi Gong can be classified as "hard" or "gentle" gong. The "hard" belongs to martial art; the "gentle" refers to health preservation or "Qi Gong Therapy."

Qi Gong can also be divided into "moving" (moving externally and calm internally) and "calm" (calm externally and moving internally).

TAI CHI: Tai Chi consists of movement and exercise routines designed to balance the energies within the body as well as the mind. Tai Chi can bring a wide range of health benefits to the muscular, skeletal and circulatory systems. Flowing movements serve as moving meditation that reduces stress and provides a way to cultivate body and mind.

Physical Activity to Combat Fatigue

Fatigue is a common side effect of cancer treatments. It is important that you let your team know when you are tired and how tired you are so that medications and transfusions can be given if appropriate. You may have to manage your fatigue by making some adjustments to your routine. Prioritize your tasks and make sure you are doing the most important tasks while you still have energy. Learn to say "no." Learn to accept help offered from family and friends, or ask for the help you need.

Eat foods high in nutritional value and maintain an exercise program. When women do not feel well, they often stop exercising altogether, in turn compromising the immune system. This can cause an increase in shoulder contracture risk (if undergoing radiation), increasing fatigue and may contribute to depression. Research shows that maintaining exercise (such as walking, weight training, stationary bike riding or yoga) will increase energy levels, flexibility, decrease depression and decrease the risk for infections or complications during cancer treatments. Taking only very short naps during the day improves night-time quality of sleep and also helps improve energy levels.

Physical Therapy to Treat Skin Changes and Scarring

Various changes in skin texture and color can be expected when undergoing surgery, radiation and/or chemotherapy. All inflammations, blisters and rashes should immediately be brought to the attention of your physician. It is also important to follow good personal hygiene during treatment, especially brushing your teeth and using a good lotion daily (e.g., Eucerin or Keri) unless contraindicated.

Most skin changes fall into the categories of dry skin, changes in skin pigmentation and infection. For people undergoing radiation therapy, a physical therapist can teach specific daily stretches, which should be done for three to five years after radiation. If radiation-induced skin changes occur, stop all stretches until your skin has healed.

Physical therapy is also important for scar tissue management after surgery. During treatment, alcohol-based products, harsh clothing (e.g., wool), sun exposure, hot baths and certain preparations (e.g., deodorants) may contribute to skin problems and be contraindicated. These should be avoided. Over the counter moisturizers and sunscreens can be helpful.

Lymphedema

Lymphedema is an abnormal accumulation of lymphatic fluid (water and protein) in the soft tissues of the body. It is usually due to an obstruction of the lymphatic system. In breast cancer patients, lymphedema can occur in the arm, hand and/or chest wall of the side of the body that had surgery. Factors contributing to the onset of lymphedema include axillary lymph node dissection and/or radiation therapy. Removal of lymph nodes causes a decreased rate of flow of the lymphatic fluid as it passes through the remaining nodes. Radiation to the chest wall and armpit causes scarring in the lymph vessels, which also slows down the rate of flow of the lymph system in this region. These changes allow lymph fluid to accumulate within the vessels and tissue spaces.

Over time, the fluid accumulates to the point that the skin is actually stretched. This may be the first symptom of lymphedema. Other early symptoms include heaviness, weakness, tingling, numbness, achiness, decreased flexibility in the hand or wrist and pain anywhere in the affected arm. Some women do not experience any symptoms while others have severe complaints. Initially, the swelling will fluctuate with activity. Many people believe that since the swelling goes away with rest that they do not need treatment. However, this is exactly when treatment should be started. If caught in the very early stages, treatment is less time-consuming and results are obtained much more quickly.

Lymphedema may occur at any time following breast cancer treatment. Some women develop symptoms within the first year and others more than twenty years later. Infections involving the affected extremity may also trigger the onset of lymphedema. The risk of developing lymphedema after breast surgery or radiation varies widely depending on the type of treatment and the patient's body. Only a small percentage of breast cancer patients

Reducing the Risk of Lymphedema

❧

- Avoid any type of trauma to the affected arm (bruising, cuts, sunburn or other burns, sports injuries, insect bites and animal scratches).

- Use an electric razor rather than a safety razor to avoid nicks.

- Do not wear tight jewelry or clothes on the affected arm/hand.

- Avoid cutting cuticles when manicuring hands.

- Avoid injections, blood draws and blood pressure readings in the affected arm (though it may be necessary to have blood drawn from this arm during chemotherapy so that the drugs can be injected into the unaffected arm).

- Monitor your affected arm and chest wall daily for signs of infection (cellulitis). If infection is suspected, contact your health care provider immediately.

- Maintain body weight for reduction in breast cancer recurrence and lymphedema prevention. Avoid tobacco, alcohol and salt.

- Slowly build up strength in the affected arm. Strength training is important for arms and legs two to three times per week. Avoid straining by not lifting a weight that is too heavy; lifting something heavy before the arm is ready may trigger lymphedema.

- Get regular aerobic exercise. Walk, swim or bike at least three to five times per week. Start out with a few minutes and gradually build up to sixty minutes each session.

- Do your shoulder stretches daily for five years after radiation therapy to prevent radiation-induced fibrosis of the shoulder.

develop severe lymphedema, but many women experience mild symptoms, especially following significant arm activity.

It is recommended that patients see a physical therapist after surgery to learn ways to prevent lymphedema and other postsurgery problems. Regaining full motion and strength in the arm, improving postural awareness and preventing infection are the best options for decreasing the risk of developing lymphedema.

You will need to take special care of the affected arm for the rest of your life, so learn how to prevent injuries and infections and what to do should one occur.

Lymphedema is best treated when caught early, so call your doctor at the first sign of swelling or infection. If the lymphedema is caused by infection, your doctor will prescribe appropriate antibiotics (some women carry a prescription with them when they travel). If the lymphedema is not caused by infection, ask for a referral to a physical therapist, and a treatment plan will be determined using methods that could include manual lymphatic drainage, bandaging, compression garments and exercises.

Physical therapists, occupational therapists and massage therapists treat lymphedema. Most patients are referred to these specialists by surgeons or oncologists. As long as you have physical therapy/occupational therapy/ rehabilitation benefits as part of your insurance coverage, and a licensed therapist provides the treatment, the services should be covered. It is important to remember that there are lifelong steps that you can take to prevent lymphedema. However, some people may be more prone to developing lymphedema and it is a manageable condition with treatment and proper self-care.

My breast cancer journey has been a passage marked by small triumphs and milestones of love. At the start of my treatment, I set a goal of exercising every day. I was proud when I could tell my oncologist on the afternoon of chemotherapy that I had run around Green Lake that morning. When I decided it was time to shave off my fast-falling hair, my son joined me and sheared his long, curly mane for a donation to Locks of Love. I walked with my daughter around the track at Husky Stadium to help her become one of the top fundraisers for the University of Washington's Relay for Life. My husband went with me to every chemo appointment, shared each decision and was ever patient with my complaints. Friends and family collaborated to send me flowers each week and hired a house cleaner. Each little victory and each act of caring got me through a week, a month, a year and, finally, to a brighter day.

—Nole Ann Ulery-Horsey, diagnosed in 2005 at age 53

༄

CHAPTER 15

Follow-up Care and Survivorship

Follow-up Care

Completing cancer treatment means having mastered a new language, finished various therapies and managed any side effects that may have arisen. Regular follow-up exams are important and continue after breast cancer treatment. These checkups usually include exams of the chest and breasts, underarms and neck. Annual mammograms, pap smears and gynecologic exams are also part of follow-up care.

There are several tests that are not normally considered standard follow-up procedures for breast cancer, but they may be recommended in some circumstances. These tests include complete blood tests (*blood counts* and liver and kidney function tests), bone scans, radiologic imaging of the liver and breast cancer tumor marker tests (which is also a blood test).

Having had cancer in one breast gives you a higher-than-average risk of developing cancer in the other breast. Breast self-examination, checking both the treated area and the other breast, should be done monthly. Recently, MRI has been shown to be effective in screening patients at high risk for breast cancer. Some patients may benefit from MRI in addition to traditional mammography for follow-up screening of both breasts.

Tell your doctor about other physical problems if they occur, including pain, loss of appetite, changes in menstrual periods, skin reddening or thickening, new lumps or nipple discharge. Most symptoms do not turn out to be related to breast cancer, and your doctor can reassure you about them.

Survivorship

All patients look forward to finishing their treatments. However, it is not unusual for patients to find their feelings changing as the last treatment appointment approaches. For many people, treatment means fighting their cancer. Even though they understand the treatment has accomplished its purpose, they feel that if they stop, they will be vulnerable to cancer's return.

Treatment time can be so occupied with medical appointments, work and families, that emotions surface only when treatment is complete. It is useful to talk about these feelings with others, such as your physician and nurse, other patients or your family. Some people find that their efforts to live a healthy lifestyle help them to feel that they are still doing something to help themselves to remain cancer-free.

You and those around you may expect life to return to "normal," but life is not the same as before your diagnosis. You may still be experiencing fatigue or other side effects for some time after ending treatment. You may find it difficult to do the work you used to do. You may find your illness affects employment or your insurance. If you do experience problems, remember that you are not alone. Thousands of other patients have gone before you, and their experiences can help you handle concerns that arise. Many support groups welcome breast cancer survivors. Creating a place for cancer in your life but keeping cancer in its place is a task of survivorship.

I had no symptoms of being ill so I was lucky that the cancer was caught by a mammogram. I prayed to God, talked with my Pastor and friends and obeyed my doctor's orders. I joined a breast cancer support group which continues to give me great support as a survivor. Since my diagnosis, I've been blessed with good health and I still get my annual mammogram.

—Johnnie Mae Davis, diagnosed in 1986 at age 63

❦

CHAPTER 16

Recurrence and/or Distant Disease: Dealing with Mortality

Since most breast cancers are detected early, and treatment for later stage cancers has improved over the past decade, there has been a significant reduction in *mortality* due to breast cancer. The death rates from breast cancer declined significantly between 1992 and 1996, with the largest decreases among younger individuals. But for a significant number of people, breast cancer will be a lifelong battle, and for some it will take their life earlier than anyone would want.

Consequently, after a diagnosis of breast cancer, fear that the disease will return or will lead to death are difficult worries to erase. But while a breast cancer patient can never be 100 percent certain that the disease is cured forever, the likelihood of future recurrence decreases with time elapsed from the initial diagnosis.

All patients hope that, once breast cancer treatment is completed, the disease will never return. In fact, as the time arrives for follow-up tests, some of the original anxiety felt at diagnosis may return. It is impossible to return to the innocence of "it cannot happen to me." These follow-up tests are important so that if breast cancer recurs treatment may begin again. Initially, it is a common fear that recurrence means a death sentence, but this is not always the case. Breast cancer recurrence and/or advanced stage disease may mean several things, so it is important to understand the differences.

LOCAL RECURRENCE: This means cancer has returned at or near the same site where it was originally found, or, in the case of those who had breast-conserving therapy, cancer appears again in the same breast. Treatment is often the same approach taken with the initial breast cancer: surgery, chemotherapy, endocrine therapy, radiation therapy. While this means a return to treatment, it is likely that treatment will be effective for some time, resulting in a hopefully long, disease-free survival.

LOCALLY ADVANCED BREAST CANCER: This means cancer that was diagnosed at a more advanced stage, and it often responds to combined modality treatment. It carries a higher risk of recurrence than a less extensive cancer at diagnosis. Over time it may recur locally or even spread to distant locations. If that happens, appropriate treatment would be offered to manage symptoms and prolong life; this treatment may continue for many years.

METASTATIC BREAST CANCER (STAGE IV): Metastatic breast cancer may have involved distant sites at the time of the initial cancer diagnosis, or the spread to distant sites might be identified some time (often many years) after the initial breast cancer treatment is complete. Even in this situation, it has been reported that a small but not irrelevant fraction of patients can be cured or remain in long-term survival with complete remission.

Coping with Recurrence

Each person's course of recurrent or metastatic breast cancer is diverse, variable and largely unpredictable. Knowing this can be frustrating when making long-term plans, yet this knowledge is also a source of hope. Many women live with advanced disease for a number of years, often well beyond statistical medical predictions. Some see their illness as a chronic condition that allows for new meanings and shifting priorities. Living fully, in the face of uncertainty, becomes the focus.

So whether you are experiencing fear of cancer recurrence or actually dealing with recurrent or metastatic breast cancer, this can be a time to examine philosophical and spiritual issues that we all often avoid or postpone, such as issues of mortality. It is not unusual for those who have been forced to face these issues to talk about how important and valuable the process was for them. People often say, "I sure did not want my cancer, but my life is so much better now than before because of the ways my experience has changed my outlook." They note how their priorities have changed and how this has freed them from many unnecessary concerns.

People come to this emotional resolution in different ways. Some have a spiritual base that can help them deal with meaning of life and mortality issues. Others find answers in literature or by talking to friends, family members or a counselor. This can also be a time when the understanding of others in similar circumstances, as in a support group, can be of great help.

Discussing disease and death-related concerns within your closest relationships can be a difficult and delicate process, while in a group of empathetic peers there is often freedom of expression and sharing. It seems that people find it important to identify what matters to them most, what gives hope or meaning to their life and what their own personal truth is. When advanced breast cancer no longer responds to the treatments available and the side effects of treatment are more difficult to deal with than the cancer itself, supportive care is very important and allows the patient and family to use the time ahead of them well.

Palliative Care/Hospice

Even before breast cancer becomes a life-threatening illness, attention to comfort and quality of life is important. In the setting of metastatic disease, one reason to offer treatment is to prolong life, but another goal is to achieve a life of an acceptable quality, so symptom control is equally important. When the goal of cancer treatment is no longer curative, it is imperative that we use good pain and symptom management to improve quality of life.

Hospice care has traditionally provided excellent symptom control. The term *hospice* was originally used to describe a place of shelter and rest for ill or fatigued travelers on long journeys. Hospice focuses on *palliative* treatment, relieving symptoms and improving quality of life, as opposed to curative treatment. It seeks to provide a pain-free, dignified life in patients' homes, hospitals and other health care settings. Hospice services are provided by a team of caregivers who work with the patient's physician and may include a nurse, social worker, home health aide, chaplain and/or volunteer. Medical services, emotional support, spiritual and other counseling and practical services are offered. Hospice helps to support family and friends in providing day-to-day patient care wherever the patient is.

Hospice services are usually covered by Medicare, Medicaid and many private insurance companies, but qualifying for payment may require the patient to stop certain medical care that is not entirely focused on symptom control. For this reason, hospice programs have traditionally offered this kind of support only for people in the last phase of *terminal* illness. From an insurance reimbursement standpoint, this phase has generally been accepted as when someone has six months or less to live and is foregoing curative treatment. In breast cancer, because one can live with metastatic disease for a long time, it is difficult to determine when one has reached the last phase of the illness or when to stop some types of medical care.

Waiting to start hospice care has meant that most patients do not benefit from this excellent form of symptom management and end-of-life planning. The average length of hospice care has dropped to thirty-six days, often not enough time to get symptoms managed or for the patient and family members to be emotionally prepared for death. To deal with this divide between excellent symptom management and waiting until very near the end of life to start this type of care, health care providers, insurance companies and organizations like Last Acts and the Robert Wood Johnson Foundation have come up with innovative ways to provide palliative care at the time the patient and her family members need it. Since there are still reimbursement issues surrounding this type of care while continuing cancer treatment, even if the treatment is focused just on managing symptoms, not all insurers cover palliative care. But there may be ways to access the care without individual cost. Consult with your physician, nurse or social worker to find out what is available in your community.

"Courage"

Chapter 17

ॐ

The Psychological Impact of Breast Cancer: Emotions, Personal Relationships, Sexuality and Support Groups

Emotions

The diagnosis of cancer can create an overwhelming experience of fear, panic or emotional shutdown. Many women say that they never heard another word after the doctor said, "I'm sorry, this is cancer." Other feelings may come and go with disconcerting regularity. There are so many ups and downs that those who work with cancer patients think of it as the "emotional roller coaster" everyone rides during the cancer experience. There may be anger, depression, anxiety and a sense of being helpless, powerless or out of control. There may also be extreme feelings of vulnerability, betrayal by your body or of unfairness, as in, "Why me?" Above all, the overriding emotion is fear: fear of treatment, fear of mutilation and fear of death.

Another emotion rarely acknowledged is grief: grief for the sense of yourself as a healthy person. Most of us carry this sense of self and seldom acknowledge it until something goes wrong with our health, when that image of ourselves is destroyed. Suddenly, we are very vulnerable! There are different kinds of grief for different losses, and cancer, with its treatment, generates so many losses. Women grieve for the loss of a breast or hair. Some will even grieve for the loss of menstrual periods.

Grief can cause many emotional responses, which will need to be assimilated and processed, not only by the patient but also by family members and friends. Often, patients will not recognize these emotions as being grief-related and are surprised, relieved and validated to hear them described as such. Many women need to give themselves permission to grieve and to express sorrow or anger. Families that can cry together and help each other grieve are most able to cope with and adjust to the rigors of treatment.

The immediate need for information and clarity about the disease and its treatment often forces women to delay their response to the emotions they are experiencing. Feelings are set aside in order to cope with the task at hand: making the right treatment decisions, starting treatment and trying to maintain some semblance of normalcy amid the chaos. Signs of repressed emotions may be mistaken for great coping skills early on, and families are often confused and anxious if a patient needs to process the reality of having cancer after the treatment ends.

Your health care team is familiar with all of the emotional effects of the cancer experience and they will be able to talk with you themselves to reassure you that these feelings are all normal, or they will refer you to professional cancer counselors. Most cancer treatment centers have counseling assistance, breast cancer support groups, educational facilities and the ability to put you in touch with other cancer patients in similar situations to help normalize your experience. Do take advantage of these options; they are available for the asking. You will be glad you did!

It is not unusual for patients to feel anxiety or depression as they deal with so many changes and so much uncertainty. This is not a sign of weakness, but rather is a normal reaction to an extraordinary situation that has overwhelmed a person's resources. It is important to let your medical caregivers know if you feel that depression or anxiety is interfering with your life. Often these feelings are a signal that you may not have allowed yourself sufficient time or opportunities to express your feelings. Or you may need more assistance and support to meet your needs. Talking with a counselor a few times often gives patients an opportunity to identify troubling feelings that need to be expressed, to receive reassurance that their feelings and reactions to their illness and treatments are very normal and to find more support. Talking with someone you feel really understands your situation can also provide much relief.

Many patients have found antidepressant medications to be very helpful during this difficult time. Patients sometimes resist taking "yet another medication," and others think that admitting to needing an antidepressant represents a weakness or a failure. However, these medications can be a valuable tool to help women manage their feelings more effectively. Women have reported that the medications gave them a way of evening out their emotions and finding the energy to cope more effectively with their situation.

Family and Children

For some women, a great concern is how their illness will affect their children. The tendency is to try to protect children by withholding information. This usually does not work well, as children are extremely sensitive and pick up family concerns. They may seem disinterested, but they overhear conversations and phone calls and are alerted by changes in their normal schedule. What helps children to cope best is being told the truth in an age-appropriate way and being able to trust that they will be kept informed. Children are amazingly resilient and can tolerate tough situations if they feel included in events, are told what they can do to help, are reassured that they in no way caused the problem, are reassured about how their schedule will continue and are told who will be available to take care of them if a parent is unavailable. It helps children to meet your doctor, to see where you go for treatments and to know that they can help by playing quietly or by drawing you a picture.

Parents need to make certain that they have the information for themselves and have reached a certain level of comfort and acceptance before trying to reassure a child. If a family is unduly anxious or fearful, this fear and anxiety will be transmitted to a child in ways that are often not obvious. Keep the lines of communication open and your antennae clear to best meet your child's ongoing emotional needs during this time of crisis in the household. Some books to help you with your children's concerns are listed in Appendix C, Publications.

Most children are quite curious about the physical signs of breast cancer treatment. Some will want to see their mother's surgical site and may be comfortable touching it if allowed to do so. One patient told her little girl that "Mommy had an 'owie' there and the doctor had to remove her breast to make her feel better." Other explanations, such as why Mommy does not have any hair, can be offered in the same way.

Lastly, a child's age plays a part in how well they understand and accept what is happening in the home or to the parent. Preschool children tend to have difficulty if Mom is not as available emotionally to them, yet they do respond well to other adults with whom they have a relationship. Interestingly, preschoolers tend to accept the loss of hair or of a breast quite matter-of-factly, and they are often not bothered if Mom does not wear her wig or her prosthesis. Older children, however, are often very conscious of hair loss, wanting Mom to wear head coverings, such as scarves, turbans, hats or wigs, and they definitely want Mom to wear her prosthesis.

Adolescence is the most problematic age for a parent to have cancer. It is a difficult time at best, and a time when children are starting to seek their own identity and to figure out their place in the world outside of the family. A family crisis at this time can disrupt this process. We often expect more help and understanding from older children, and they are unable or unwilling to provide it. Typically, adolescents want less time with their family, not more! They will certainly rebel if given additional chores or tasks stemming from Mom's need for increased help. This is also a time when older children, especially teenagers, want conformity in every way. They may hate that Mom does not have any hair, and they may insist that she not pick them up from activities or be seen with them unless she looks good. For moms of teenagers, that means full makeup, wig and prosthesis. All of this is normal, but it can also be painful for the parent who expected more understanding or cooperation. If a family is dysfunctional prior to the cancer diagnosis, the dysfunction will be increased by the stress of the cancer experience. These families will benefit from counseling, a support group or some additional attention by health care professionals.

Questions about how to talk about your illness may come up with your spouse or partner as well. Again, talking as openly and honestly as possible works best. Sometimes it is easiest for you to initiate this by saying something like, "We have been focused on me and my illness; how is all this for you? What has been hardest for you? What is scariest?" Hearing their concerns may open communication by letting them know you recognize that they are affected by your illness as well. Cancer affects the whole family, and managing it works best if the family copes together. Sometimes it helps to think of the family as a team. Coping takes teamwork.

Because each family member has special roles, you need to keep your signals straight by having regular team meetings to check how the game is going and to prepare for the next scrimmage. Often, what is hard for family members is seeing you suffer and feeling helpless to do anything meaningful to make things better for you. You can help them best by letting them know realistic ways in which they can support you.

One of the things most women find very supportive is for their partner or another close person to really listen to them. You may find that it helps to tell the person how useful that is, letting him or her know that you need someone to listen and understand as you sort out your feelings. Your partner or friend needs to know that this kind of listening and understanding is a valuable gift. Your knowing they understand and care can give you the strength to handle difficult situations.

Caregiving by Family and Friends

CHANGING ROUTINES: The whole family feels the impact of breast cancer. Most hospitals have social workers available to support and counsel the patient and the family. Other family members need to share the workload, but the patient should be encouraged to continue to do as much as possible. Friends of the family may also be asked to provide support and assistance—more than flowers and a get-well card. There are many ways family and friends can help a breast cancer patient undergoing treatment (see next page, "What You Can Do to Help").

TAKING CARE OF THE CAREGIVER: Caregivers and family members can become overwhelmed, and they need to take care of themselves as well as the patient. They need to determine their abilities and limits and then make genuine offers of assistance that are not undue sacrifices. Assess the situation and involve others to assist with the caregiving when you have reached your limits. No one can continue to provide ongoing support unless they recharge their own batteries once in a while.

Body Image and Sexuality

Cancer and cancer treatments can be very desexualizing, and breast cancer patients may experience several types of body changes: changes in or loss of the breast due to surgery, lymphedema (swelling) of the arm after node dissection, loss of hair from chemotherapy and changes in sexual functioning due to vaginal dryness caused by chemotherapy or menopausal symptoms (like hot flashes). Women who have endured total body hair loss, weight gain or loss, extreme fatigue or mastectomy often experience lowered self-esteem and a damaged self-image.

Sexual intimacy during treatment often takes a back seat to these very real side effects. Many women also feel unacceptable after surgery, and they imagine that their partner feels the same way. Women may also be focused on their own needs, their treatment and its side effects, and partners may experience this as a withdrawal. For their part, partners sometimes hesitate to initiate physical contact.

Remember that you are both coping with a shift in roles while adjusting to many changes. You, as the patient, may have feelings of insecurity and guilt. Experiencing these difficult feelings is a normal part of the coping process. Allow yourself time to adapt to the changes in your body, your self-image and your feelings about yourself, and allow yourself time to reestablish physical intimacy with your partner. Partners can help by providing support, love and affection in the form of frequent hugs and kisses, which may help the patient feel more comfortable with physical or sexual intimacy. A supportive partner offering unconditional love can assure the patient that the intangible personal qualities that make up a large part of the relationship are still intact.

It is crucial to inform yourself about the possible body changes you may experience and to communicate your questions and feelings to your health care provider and/or your partner. If you cannot talk openly about your feelings, emotional wounds may continue to exist long after physical wounds have healed. On the physical side, most physicians can offer treatments to minimize or treat the worst of the menopausal symptoms. Emotionally, discussing your feelings with your partner and expressing your desire for physical affection are necessary for maintaining closeness. Let your partner know that direct communication is important to you. Encourage conversation by sharing your own thoughts and feelings, but recognize that timing is important in creating the right environment for such a discussion. Consider a family conference with a qualified cancer counselor to help facilitate such a conversation. A counselor can also help you to grapple with these very personal feelings and to maintain self-esteem.

Talking with other women with breast cancer, either one-on-one or in a support group, can also help. Intimacy issues created by cancer and its treatment are a recurring topic in breast cancer support groups, as well as in caregiver support groups. Openly addressing and discussing feelings and fears with a counselor or support group can help in coping with emotional and physical changes associated with treatment.

Appendix B, Organizations and Resources, and Appendix C, Publications, list many support options. For instance, *Spinning Straw into Gold*, by Ronnie Kaye, has a good discussion about adjusting to a new body image, and *Breast Cancer Husband*, by Marc Silver, is a good resource for partners to consult.

What You Can Do to Help

&.

- Listen to and respect your loved one's feelings.
- Treat the patient with respect.
- Tolerate the mood swings, anxiety, fears and tears! Allow for an expression of these feelings and find an outlet for yourself.
- Help the patient to prioritize and recognize that change in routine is inevitable. No one can do all they used to while undergoing chemotherapy or radiation treatment.
- Stay in touch, send a funny card or visit.
- Encourage others to stay in touch.
- Prepare meals and encourage others to do the same. Let the patient know who will be bringing meals and on which days.
- Offer to do household chores.
- Offer to run errands for the patient.
- Offer to take the patient to doctor visits.
- Organize a care team.
- Water the plants.
- Do the laundry.
- Do the grocery shopping.
- Take one day at a time. Stay in the present and help the patient do the same.

Support Groups

Many cancer patients find strength and support through sharing their thoughts and feelings with other women who have been through a common experience. Support groups can be helpful for deriving emotional support and sharing information.

Frequently led by knowledgeable professionals, support groups often include an educational focus as well as offering the opportunity for open discussion of a whole range of issues, from treatment to communication with family members. Sometimes a support group may be the one place a patient feels openly comfortable talking about these issues. Many patients think of their support group time as their special time, and the support group may actually become extended family.

One thing to consider while sharing experiences is that every person is different. Treatment given to one person may not be appropriate for another. Responses to treatment will also differ, so that what someone else experiences will not necessarily be predictive of what you will experience.

When looking for a support group, ask your nurse, social worker or doctor about available programs in your area. Once you find a group, it is a good idea to call before attending to confirm format, times and other information. See Appendix B, Organizations and Resources, for a list of support groups.

Beyond Diagnosis and Treatment

It's really not over when it's over! No one emerges from the breast cancer experience the same as when she entered it. It takes a long while for a woman to process and integrate this frightening experience into the big picture of her life, and for some, life is never the same. There may be some emotional backlash when treatment has ended. It is then that some women first begin to deal with the reality that they had cancer and to face the emotional work that accompanies the losses that cancer brings. This may be difficult for friends and family to understand. After all, it's over, you did it, you survived!

Surprisingly, many women find that post-treatment is the time they need a breast cancer support group or individual counseling. Treatment offers real security; the end of treatment can often escalate fears. For the patient's support people, support does not end with treatment but continues as long as necessary, sometimes for the rest of a person's life. Take care of yourself: Take in a movie, go for a walk, get a massage, even take the day off if possible. Remember, you will get through this! And when you do, reward yourself. You deserve something special even if it is just a weekend away.

"Wake"

—Penny Lewis, Breast Cancer Survivor

CHAPTER 18

Menopause
without Hormones

Chemotherapy and some endocrine treatments often cause the sudden onset of menopause. Although estrogen replacement therapy is used in the general menopausal population, estrogen support for breast cancer survivors is controversial and not recommended by most oncologists. Women may struggle as they try to find ways to manage the associated side effects. Hot flashes, sleep disturbances, mood swings and vaginal dryness are obvious symptoms that women report, while osteoporosis and heart disease are silent, yet important, long-term effects.

The following suggestions may help ease the side effects of menopause. As always, it is recommended that you review the suggested activities with your health care providers to ensure that they are right for you.

Hot Flashes and Night Sweats

Hot flashes are sudden, intense episodes in which the skin's surface heats up and sweating occurs to cool the body down. They can happen during the day or at night, and they vary in frequency and severity from woman to woman.

LIFESTYLE CHANGES TO MANAGE HOT FLASHES:

- Avoid symptom triggers. Strong emotions, caffeine, alcohol, cayenne or other spices, tight clothing and hot weather can all trigger reactions.

- Exercise. Walk, swim, dance, bicycle or row for twenty to thirty minutes each day.

- Stay cool. Use well-ventilated rooms and fans. Dress in layers made of natural fabrics. Drink at least eight glasses of cool water per day.
- Reduce your stress. Try deep, slow abdominal breathing, six to eight breaths per minute. Practice for fifteen minutes each morning and evening, and use the technique whenever you feel a flash coming on. Also consider daily meditation, prayer, Tai Chi or yoga.

SOME CONVENTIONAL TREATMENTS FOR HOT FLASHES:

- Low-dose antidepressants from the SSRI (selective seratonin reuptake inhibitors) family. For example, retilafaxine (Effexor), fluoxetine (Prozac) and poroxitine (Paxil).
- Gabapentine (Neurontin). A drug used to treat seizure disorders and some types of pain. Recent studies have shown it can significantly reduce hot flashes in some women.
- Medroxy progesterone (Megace). A hormone sometimes used in high doses to treat breast cancer. At lower doses it can help hot flashes. Weight gain can be a side effect.
- Bellergal. A combination of drugs that includes belladonna and can help alleviate hot flashes. Sedation can be a bothersome side effect.
- Clonidine. A blood pressure medication that comes as a pill or a patch. Low blood pressure can be a side effect.

SOME ALTERNATIVE TREATMENTS FOR HOT FLASHES:

Although more research is needed concerning alternative treatments for menopausal symptoms, such treatments may help some women. Check with your health care provider before using any of these remedies.

- Phytoestrogens. Weak plant estrogens found in soy, red clover and flax. Can have weak estrogenic and/or anti-estrogenic effects. Studies on menopausal effects are mixed.
- Black cohosh (remifemin). Studies on hot flashes show mixed results.

Menopausal Insomnia

Continual interruption of sleep makes life difficult. Night sweats and a racing heart, which are associated with menopause, can wake you up at night, and other factors can keep you from easily going back to sleep. In addition to the previous suggestions for dealing with hot flashes, the following suggestions may be helpful in dealing with insomnia.

STRATEGIES FOR AVOIDING OR ALLEVIATING INSOMNIA:

- Use bed linens made of natural fabric.
- Keep the bedroom temperature between sixty-four and sixty-six degrees.
- Avoid caffeine, excess alcohol and simple sugars (e.g., candy, cake) before bedtime. Caffeine and alcohol use can affect some individuals' sleep for days after consumption.
- Think of your bedroom as your place for peace, relaxation and sleep.
- Try to leave work and other discussions in the office or other rooms of your home.
- Consider stress counseling.
- Take a warm shower or bath at bedtime or after waking during your sleep time.
- Try to develop a routine of going to bed and getting up at the same times of the day. If you have not fallen asleep after twenty to thirty minutes, get up and leave the bedroom.
- Consider complementary treatments for insomnia, which can include chamomile tea, oat straw, nettle tea and valerian (*Valeriana officinalis*), although the latter can be habit forming.
- Consider Western treatments for insomnia. These generally include drugs in the class called benzodiazepines, such as diazepam (Valium), alprazolam (Xanax), triazolam (Halcion), temazepam (Restoril) and zolpidem (Ambien). These medications are very good at inducing sleep, but side effects can include prolonged drowsiness and the development of drug tolerance or addiction.

Mood Swings, Fear and Despair

A breast cancer diagnosis in itself can bring on feelings of helplessness and fear. The menopausal symptoms induced by treatment can then strike a double blow, adding to already heightened levels of anxiety. While each person is different, the experiences of breast cancer patients suggest some helpful ways of coping with menopausal symptoms such as mood swings, fear and despair.

STRATEGIES FOR MANAGING YOUR EMOTIONS:

- Avoid tranquilizers.
- Stay connected to your community and nourish your friendships.
- Get involved with a support group or a counselor.
- Find and practice activities that renew your spirit and your tranquility (e.g., relaxation exercises, prayer, meditation, yoga and/or slow abdominal breathing).
- Consider using homeopathic remedies. Use a naturopath to guide you in their use.

Sexuality

When ovarian production of estrogen stops or is significantly decreased, all areas of the body stimulated by estrogen undergo some change. Women may notice a decreased sex drive and an increase in vaginal dryness, which can lead to pain with penetration of the vagina.

The ability to feel pleasure from touching almost always remains. Nerves and muscles involved in the sensation of orgasm (climax) are not lost because of menopause. There are very few medications that interfere with the nerves and muscles involved in orgasm.

Keep an open mind about ways to feel sexual pleasure. Menopause may give you and your partner an opportunity to learn new ways to give and receive satisfaction. Strive to maintain open communication with your partner about the changes that are taking place. In addition, take the time to relax and become aroused and be sensitive to your level of energy. If you are too tired at the end of the day, consider making time with your partner at an earlier time in the day. Also try creating an environment that enhances your sensuality and sexuality. Consider the effects of lighting, clothing, aromas, warmth and coolness.

If sexual problems persist, be sure to talk openly to your health care provider and have a thorough pelvic exam. Counseling and support groups can help you and your partner develop better communication and reestablish your enjoyment of sexual intimacy.

Vaginal Dryness

The drop in estrogen levels at menopause can cause a decrease in the lubrication of the vagina. At the same time, the vaginal lining thins and becomes more fragile. To help combat this, avoid chemical or mechanical irritants like feminine hygiene products, keep sexually active and try water-soluble lubricants for vaginal penetration, such as Astroglide, Slippery Stuff, Imagination, Gyne-moisten, and K-Y type gels. Replens adheres to the vaginal wall and is intended to last longer. In addition, avoid any personal lubricants that contain fragrance or color, and do not use a petroleum- or oil-based product (i.e., no massage oils). The vaginal and vulvar tissue can become very thin and very easily traumatized during acts of intercourse, and any slight abrasion or break in the skin can present an opportunity for inflammation, or even possible infection.

Vaginal estrogen is sometimes prescribed in the form of creams, dissolvable tablets or a vaginal ring. Breast cancer survivors should talk to their oncology team about the safety of and correct way to use these prescription products. Only a very small amount of estrogen cream is usually needed for the relief of vaginal dryness. A low-dose estrogen ring, Estring, is less messy than creams and is minimally absorbed into the rest of the body. Do not use estrogen creams as a lubricant.

Osteoporosis

Prevention and treatment of osteoporosis in breast cancer patients involve diet, exercise, and in some women, anti-osteoporotic medications. *Osteoporosis* is a thinning of the bones due to loss of bone minerals (mainly calcium). Estrogen protects women from bone loss, which accelerates after menopause. Estrogen is an excellent drug for the prevention and treatment of osteoporosis, although it is usually avoided in breast cancer patients.

STRATEGIES FOR PREVENTING OSTEOPOROSIS:

- Calcium. The current calcium recommendation for women under 65 is 1,200 milligrams per day when estrogen or other osteoporosis preventive medications are used. Otherwise, 1,500 milligrams per day is recommended.
- Calcium-dense foods include dairy products, calcium-fortified orange juice and fortified soymilk. Very dark green vegetables and

dried beans contain calcium in smaller amounts. A large variety of calcium supplements are on the market.

- Vitamin D and magnesium. Vitamin D is necessary for the body to absorb and use calcium. Current recommendations are 400 IU per day until age 70, then 800 IU per day. In addition, magnesium at about half the dosage of calcium helps your body utilize the calcium.

- Bisphosphonates and other drugs. The bisphosphonates, alendronate (Fosmax), risedronate (Actonel) and ibandronate (Bondronat, Boniva), and the anti-estrogen raloxifene (Evista), have been approved by the Food and Drug Administration (FDA) to treat and/or prevent osteoporosis. It is well recognized that tamoxifen (Nolvadex), commonly used in the treatment of breast cancer, also has a protective effect against bone mineral loss. Several other drugs, including ralcitonin and parathyroid hormone, are currently under investigation.

- Exercise. Weight-bearing exercise is also important in building and maintaining premenopausal bone mass and improving balance. Choose activities that are muscle building and that put reasonable stress on your large bones, for example, walking, light running or jogging. You may want to consider working with a physical therapist, exercise pathologist or other provider to develop a safe, effective plan.

Heart Disease

Postmenopausal women are generally at a higher risk of heart disease, so here are some suggestions for taking care of yourself.

STRATEGIES FOR PREVENTING HEART DISEASE:

- Exercise. Develop and maintain a routine with at least twenty to thirty minutes per day of moderate exercise; it can be ten to fifteen minutes at a time. Walk, climb stairs, bicycle, dance, swim or row. Joining an organized aerobics program can sometimes provide the motivation and support to keep you going.

- Stop smoking. Smoking triples the risk of heart disease.

- Eat a wide variety of vegetables, fruits and whole grains, including soy foods in moderation, every day.

- Prepare food without frying or adding excessive amounts of oil.
- Read the labels on your food products. Avoid items with high fat and cholesterol content.
- Try to limit your diet to twenty grams or less of saturated fat per day.
- Get B vitamins from food sources or a supplement. These vitamins have a role in decreasing heart disease.
- Maintain a healthy weight. Being 20 percent or more overweight increases your risk of heart disease.

"You've Got a Friend"

🍂

Chapter 19

The Financial, Insurance and Legal Impacts of Breast Cancer

Financial Options

R esources are available for uninsured and underinsured women who have financial and health insurance difficulties.

PUBLIC ASSISTANCE: Residents of Washington State are eligible for public assistance depending on their financial resources. To obtain more information or to apply for assistance, contact a local community service office (CSO). If you have difficulty locating that office, contact the Medical Assistance Administration at (800) 562-3022 to ask for help.

BASIC HEALTH PLAN: This is a low-cost package of benefits that is available to individuals and businesses across the state. The plan is available at full cost to anyone, although the system often has a waiting list for enrollment. A sliding scale is used to adjust premiums for low-income individuals and families. For information, including specific benefits and costs, contact the Basic Health Plan at (800) 660-9840, or visit www.basichealth.hca.wa.gov.

MEDICARE: To get answers to questions regarding Medicare eligibility and enrollment, contact the Social Security Administration at (800) 772-1213, or visit www.medicare.gov.

HOSPITALS: All hospitals receive some funds from the federal government under the Hill-Burton Act to provide care to individuals with no health insurance. Women can contact the patient financial office, patient referral line or patient advocate provided by their hospital to find out about alternative resources for health coverage.

PHARMACEUTICAL COMPANIES: Some companies have needs-based programs; ask your oncology social worker about them.

NONPROFITS: The American Cancer Society and Y-ME are examples of nonprofit community groups that provide free services in such areas as transportation, prostheses, wigs and skin care. See Appendix B, Organizations and Resources, for contact information.

Insurance Coverage

Federal and state laws govern private health insurance. The rules of your health insurance plan are dependent on whether you purchase it yourself (individual plan), whether it is purchased by your employer (group health plan) or whether you are part of a self-funded plan. A self-funded health plan is exempt from state regulations. State regulations will entitle you to certain kinds of coverage.

In Washington, your health insurance options do not depend on your health status. All health plans in Washington must limit the exclusion of preexisting conditions. Your health insurance cannot be canceled because you are sick. An additional health plan cannot turn you down for coverage because of your age or health status.

UNDERSTANDING YOUR HEALTH INSURANCE: Health insurance can be categorized as one of two types of coverage: indemnity plans and managed care. Within the two types of coverage there are four types of plans: fee for service, preferred provider organizations (PPOs), point of service plans (POS) and health maintenance organizations (HMOs). No one type of health insurance is better than the other. The differences among the types of health insurance are related to your costs and how you access care. It is important to understand what type of health care coverage you have and the access rules and costs associated with it.

The place to start in understanding your health insurance coverage is your benefit booklet or certificate of coverage. The customer service department of your health insurance company will also be able to answer questions related to your benefits.

Statewide Health Insurance Benefits Advisors (SHIBA) is a statewide network of trained volunteers who help consumers and their families with questions about health insurance. The Washington State Insurance Commissioner's office sponsors this service. Volunteers in communities around the state are available to meet with consumers to discuss Medicare, Medigap (Medicare supplement) insurance, managed care, long-term care insurance, employment-related benefits, medical billing assistance and other consumer

Mandatory Breast Cancer-Related Health
Benefits in Washington State

ন্ধ্য

- Mammography screening. Disability policies covering hospital and medical expenses must cover mammography screening or diagnostic services.

- Mastectomy. No insurer may cancel or deny coverage or restrict the rates or benefits of a person who received a mastectomy or lumpectomy more than five years previously.

- Breast reconstruction. Disability policies covering hospital and medical expenses must cover breast reconstruction resulting from a mastectomy.

- In 1996, Congress passed the Health Insurance Portability and Accountability Act (HIPAA). This law and Washington's health insurance laws protect you in purchasing health insurance if you have a serious health condition.

protection issues. Call the SHIBA referral line at (800) 562-6900 to set up an interview with a volunteer.

FILING A CLAIM AND DISPUTES: IN FILING A CLAIM OR
DISPUTING A DENIED CLAIM, THE FOLLOWING
GENERAL TIPS MAY BE HELPFUL:

- Review your policy or employee benefit booklet carefully to be sure the service in question is covered.

- Follow any managed care rules, including precertification requirements and use of network providers.

- If a claim is denied, the reason for the denial should be stated in your explanation of benefits.

- If you disagree with the denial, check your policy and employee benefit booklet for the insurance company's appeal process.

- The company should be able to answer questions regarding the appeal process over the telephone.

- Your appeal should be in writing, and it may be necessary to provide information from your doctor. Be sure to keep copies of your appeal.

- If you have tried unsuccessfully to resolve a claim dispute with your insurance company, you may need to contact the Washington State Insurance Commissioner's office. The Consumer Advocacy division can be reached at (800) 562-6900. The staff will be able to advise you on how to file a complaint with their office.

MEDICARE: Currently, people 65 years or older and people with qualifying disabilities are eligible for Medicare. Certain women with advanced breast cancer may qualify under Medicare's disability eligibility. To get answers to questions regarding Medicare eligibility and enrollment, contact the Social Security Administration at (800) 772-1213, or visit www.medicare.gov. It is important to ask whether your provider accepts Medicare claims before receiving service.

MEDICAID: Medicaid is a joint state and federal health insurance program for low-income individuals with medical needs. Applications for Medicaid are made through your local community service office of the Washington State Department of Social and Health Services. It is advisable to make sure your provider accepts Medicaid reimbursement payments before being seen.

Taking Leave from Work

In 1993 the Family and Medical Leave Act (FMLA) was signed into law. It guarantees that people who work for companies with more than fifty employees can take up to twelve weeks of unpaid leave a year to care for a newborn or newly adopted child, for certain seriously ill family members, or to recover from their own serious health conditions. To find out more about this law, contact your employer's human resources department or the U.S. Department of Labor's Wage and Hour Division at (206) 553-4482.

Legal Assistance

Legal issues related to breast cancer typically fall into two general areas: (1) those involving employment, insurance and public benefits and (2) those involving basic legal matters affecting your assets and health care wishes.

EMPLOYMENT, INSURANCE AND PUBLIC BENEFITS: If disputes arise regarding employment, insurance and public benefits, they typically require independent analysis of the facts and review of applicable violations of laws.

The type of legal assistance needed depends on the issues being raised and the types of remedies being sought. When seeking legal advice, be prepared to provide a clear description of the problem with the appropriate documentation to support your position.

Finding appropriate legal counsel can be challenging. It is rare to find an attorney or legal group with special experience related to breast cancer. Fortunately, many attorneys have had experience with employment discrimination and insurance coverage issues. The Northwest Women's Law Center and county bar associations provide referrals. People with limited income may contact the Northwest Justice Project for assistance (see Appendix B, Organizations and Resources, for contact information). When selecting an attorney, always ask about their experience with similar cases and the outcomes, as well as the estimated costs.

It is always advisable to seek legal assistance prior to filing a complaint, since many legal complaints must follow state and/or federal filing guidelines. These guidelines may require adherence to strict timelines. In some cases, complaints must be filed with government agencies prior to taking other legal action. For example, employment discrimination complaints must first be filed with the U.S. Department of Health and Human Service's Office of Civil Rights (see Appendix B, Organizations and Resources, for contact information).

PERSONAL ASSETS AND HEALTH CARE WISHES: Legal instruments are available to deal with matters involving personal assets and health care wishes. The following is a basic list of legal instruments regarding health care wishes, legal and financial affairs and distribution of assets in the event of death:

- A Durable Power of Attorney for Health Care allows your designee to carry out your health care decisions if you become unable to do so yourself.

- A Durable Power of Attorney for Legal and Financial Affairs allows your designee to manage your legal and financial affairs if you are unable to do so yourself.

- A Health Care Directive outlines the medical procedures you may, or may not, want performed. These include tube feeding and life-support machines.

- Wills are used to direct where and how your assets will be distributed when you die.

Forms are available at business stationery stores, some medical facilities and private attorneys' offices. Additionally, many excellent books have been written to provide detailed information about each of these options. For title recommendations contact the American Cancer Society, ask a bookseller or check with a reference librarian at your local branch library.

I woke up to find a deep brownish stain on the upper-right side of my pajama top. I was scared. I had been laid-off from my job so I had no health insurance. I feared the worst. As I was reading the Korean newspaper, I came across an ad for free breast cancer screening, diagnosis, and treatment called the Breast and Cervical Health Program. Suddenly I felt a sign of hope. I called and was set up with an appointment for a breast biopsy, ultrasound and mammogram. When I was told of the diagnosis of cancer this was a life altering moment. My treatment included surgery, chemotherapy and reconstruction.

I want to thank the Breast and Cervical Health Program and my family. Thank you all very much.

—Mona Kim, diagnosed in 2002 at age 48

CHAPTER 20

ॐ

Research for Breast Cancer: Hope for the Future

Breast Cancer Biology

Success in breast cancer prevention, diagnosis and treatment lies in a more complete understanding of the cancer cell, including the alterations in genes and proteins that allow a cell to become malignant. Thus, much current research focuses on the biology of normal and cancerous breast cells. We are learning more about how genes influence breast cancer, and there should be rapid progress now that the human genome has been sequenced.

Oncogenes are cancer-associated genes that are found in the DNA of all cells and that play a role in normal cell growth and differentiation. Oncogenes are usually inactive in normal cells in our adult life. If they mutate, are amplified or are "turned on" inappropriately by associated regulatory genes, this can cause the runaway cell growth associated with cancer. An error of DNA replication that results in the activation of an oncogene is like pressing down on the accelerator of a car—it speeds up cell growth and division.

The presence of certain oncogenes is being used to help determine which tumors are likely to recur after surgery, to target treatments and to predict which treatments are likely to work for a given tumor. HER-2 is an important oncogene in breast and other cancers. Its presence in a breast cancer is a predictor of tumors that are more aggressive and less likely to respond to hormone therapy and some forms of chemotherapy. HER-2 is also the target of the drug trastuzumab (Herceptin), the first biologic therapy approved by the Food and Drug Administration (FDA) to be used in the treatment of breast cancer.

Tumor suppressor genes are also cancer-associated genes found in normal DNA. This class of genes acts in the opposite way of oncogenes. These genes are usually turned on in normal cells, suppressing cell growth and division and aiding in DNA repair. If a mutation or error occurs in a tumor suppressor gene, the affected cell can grow and divide in an uncontrolled manner. P53 is one of several tumor suppressor genes associated with breast cancer development.

BRCA1 and BRCA2 are two important breast cancer genes associated with a familial tendency to develop breast and ovarian cancer. These genes appear to act as tumor suppressor genes when they are functioning normally, but lose this function when they are mutated in some individuals. An error of DNA replication that results in the deactivation of a tumor suppressor gene is like letting off on the brakes of a car—it speeds up cell growth and division.

Breast Cancer Risk Factors and Genetics

Ongoing studies are investigating alterable lifestyle factors that can affect breast cancer risk. These include trials evaluating the effect of exercise and physical activity, weight gain or loss and diet on breast cancer development and recurrence.

Research into the inherited genetics of cancer continues. The two primary genes responsible for inherited breast cancer risk, BRCA1 and BRCA2, were discovered in the 1990s. Mutations in these genes are responsible for about 5 to 10 percent of all breast cancers. More recently, PTEN and CHK2 have been identified as genes that may play a role in inherited breast cancer risk in other families. It is possible that for some (if not most) women, a combination of inheritance of one or several "weaker" breast cancer genes that have not yet been discovered plays a role in their breast cancer development.

A large, long-term study now under way is trying to better define the causes of cancer. It is known as the Sister Study, and it will follow 50,000 women whose sisters (not they themselves) have had breast cancer. Over ten years, information will be gathered on environmental, lifestyle and genetic factors that may cause breast cancer. If you (or a family member) want to find out more about the Sister Study, call (877) 4-SISTER or visit www.sisterstudy.org.

Breast Cancer Prevention

Clinical trials are looking at drugs, vitamins and other supplements to prevent breast cancer. Tamoxifen was approved as a chemopreventive agent for breast cancer in the 1990s. Prevention studies of other endocrine therapies (currently used to treat breast cancer), as well as other classes of drugs, are ongoing.

The anti-estrogens tamoxifen and raloxifene are being studied as breast cancer preventive agents in the National Surgical Breast and Bowel Project's (NSABP) P-02 Study of Tamoxifen and Raloxifene (STAR) Trial. This trial has closed to accrual, and initial results show that raloxifene is as effective as tamoxifen in reducing trial participants' breast cancer risk. Both drugs reduced the risk of developing invasive breast cancer by about 50 percent. In addition, women who were assigned to take raloxifene daily and who were followed for an average of about four years had 36 percent fewer uterine cancers and 29 percent fewer blood clots than women assigned to take tamoxifen. Uterine cancers, especially endometrial cancers, are a rare but serious side effect of tamoxifen. Both tamoxifen and raloxifene are known to increase a woman's risk of blood clots.

Two international trials of aromatase inhibitors for chemoprevention of postmenopausal breast cancer are currently enrolling patients—the IBIS-II Trial and the MAP-3 (EXCEL) Trial. For further information on the EXCEL Trial, open in North America, visit www.excelstudy.com. For premenopausal women, the Southwest Oncology Group (SWOG) S0300 Trial is looking at the COX-2 inhibitor celecoxib (Celebrex) as a chemopreventive agent. Researchers are also examining synthetic retinoids (vitamin A-like compounds), like fenretinide, as preventive agents in women at high risk for developing breast cancer.

Breast Cancer Detection and Diagnosis

Until the day that breast cancer can be prevented altogether, early detection of cancer through screening techniques remains our most important tool for maximizing the chance of cure. Mammography is an excellent diagnostic tool in most women, but it lacks sensitivity in the subgroup of patients with dense or irregular breasts. New diagnostic approaches are being investigated.

MRIS: *Magnetic resonance imaging* (MRI) shows breast tissue in ways that mammograms cannot, by using a large magnet and contrast dye instead of radiation to build two- and three-dimensional pictures of the breasts. MRI screening is highly sensitive and can identify cancers not seen on mammography. MRI, in addition to mammography, has a recently proven role in screening young women with a very strong family history of breast cancer. It is under investigation as a supplemental test for screening other populations, including women with dense breasts on mammograms. MRI technology has been in widespread use for about twenty years, but only recently has been studied for breast cancer detection.

PET SCANS: PET (positron emission tomography) scans are being increasingly used to determine the extent of cancer spread both at diagnosis and at recurrence and to follow the response to treatment in advanced breast cancer patients. The most commonly used type of PET scan uses glucose (a sugar) that is tagged with a small amount of radioactivity to find areas in the body with high levels of metabolism. Usually, cancer cells have high levels of metabolism (as measured by sugar use) when compared to our normal tissues. Newer and still very much experimental PET approaches include studying other molecules tagged to radioactivity, including estrogen (which can then evaluate the hormone receptor expression of the tumor throughout the body) and thymidine (which can look at DNA production, required for cell division).

GENE ANALYSIS: Genomic (molecular) profiling may be the future for classifying breast cancers and deciding the best treatment for individual patients. In the past, breast cancer patients have been treated based on relatively simple guidelines, such as tumor size, presence of lymph node involvement and whether the cancers were hormone receptor–positive. Today, with a sample of the patient's tumor cells, we can look at a cancer's gene expression profile using a microarray, in which thousands of genes can be viewed at once to determine the degree to which they are being expressed in a given cancer.

Two gene-profiling assays designed to predict breast cancer recurrence in early stage breast cancer have recently been approved in the United States. These are the Oncotype Dx 21-gene Recurrence Score Assay and the Mammaprint 70-gene Profiling Assay. These tests, and others like them that are in development, may help the physician and the patient make a decision about whether to undergo adjuvant chemotherapy. Much research is being done to validate and perfect these assays for predicting breast cancer recurrence and to develop tests that can also predict which treatments will work best.

CIRCULATING TUMOR CELLS: Breast cancer cells, whether in the breast or in distant locations, can be shed into the bloodstream. A recently approved test called CellSearch was designed to detect the presence of circulating tumor cells (CTCs) in the peripheral blood of cancer patients. CTC analysis may prove to be a powerful new tool in cancer diagnosis and in following response to treatment.

Breast Cancer Surgery and Radiation Therapy

Breast cancer treatment strategies are constantly evolving, with the goal of achieving maximum benefit for the patient with minimum toxicity and side effects. Breast surgeons have demonstrated through careful clinical trials that reducing the extent of the surgery in appropriately selected breast cancer patients (breast conservation surgery or lumpectomy) can achieve comparable survival results when compared to more extensive surgery (mastectomy).

SENTINAL LYMPH NODE MAPPING: Through a technique called *senti*nel lymph node mapping, surgeons have also been successful in reducing the number of axillary lymph node dissections performed in breast cancer patients. If this sentinel lymph node is free of cancer, the chance of cancer involvement farther up the lymph node chain is very low. In such a case, the remaining lymph nodes are left intact, and a full axillary lymph node dissection is avoided. If the sentinel node contains tumor cells, a full axillary dissection is performed to determine the extent of the spread to the other lymph nodes.

BREAST RECONSTRUCTION: Advances in reattaching blood vessels (microvascular surgery) have led to improvements in breast reconstruction. A new tissue reconstruction technique called a DIEP (deep inferior epigastric perforator, also called a free flap) is a modified version of the more standard TRAM flap (transverse rectus abdominus myocutaneous flap) breast reconstruction surgery. The advantage of the DIEP procedure is that the abdominal muscles are left in place.

PARTIAL BREAST RADIATION: An experimental technique for breast radiation currently under investigation is called partial breast radiation. This type of radiation focuses on only part of the breast tissue, the area around the lumpectomy site. Usually, more intensive radiation is delivered over a shorter time period compared to standard external beam radiation.

BRACHYTHERAPY: This is a type of partial breast radiation that is internal. There are several different techniques for brachytherapy, including a balloon that can be inserted in the operating room to deliver radiation, radiation seeds that are implanted into the breast and external catheters that can be temporarily placed around the lumpectomy scar and hooked up one to two times a day to deliver focused radiation. A large, randomized national clinical trial by the National Surgical Breast and Bowel Project (NSABP B-39/ RTOG 0413) started enrollment in early 2006. It will compare conventional whole breast radiation to experimental partial breast radiation in selected women with early stage breast cancer.

Systemic Therapy

In the field of medical oncology, many promising new systemic breast cancer treatments are being developed and investigated in clinical trials. The best way to find out about clinical trials that might be appropriate for you is to talk to your health care team. Two online resources are Centerwatch's listing of clinical trials that are actively recruiting (www.centerwatch.com) and the National Institutes of Health's clinical trials database (www.clinicaltrials.gov), which allows searches for clinical trials by disease type and stage, treatment type and your geographic location.

CHEMOTHERAPY: Albumin-bound paclitaxel (Abraxane) is a new formulation of paclitaxel (Taxol) that was approved for the treatment of metastatic breast cancer in 2005. Advantages of this new formulation include that it dissolves well in water (which Taxol does not), which means it can be given more quickly and without many of the premedications traditionally given with Taxol to prevent allergic reactions to the substance (Cremophor) that is needed to keep Taxol (but not Abraxane) in solution. By taking advantage of the tumor's increased need for nutrients, particularly the protein albumin, drug delivery is made easier. This drug is now under study in early stage breast cancer, as are other related drugs with innovative modifications of the Taxol compound.

Epothilones are a new class of chemotherapy agent that are related to but distinct from the taxanes, Taxol and docetaxel (Taxotere). Both classes of drugs bind to tubulins in dividing cells and prevent cell division. Several versions of epothilones are in clinical trials. Ixabepilone, the epothilone that is furthest along in clinical development, has shown promise in advanced breast cancer.

Another chemotherapy drug that may prove to be useful in breast cancer treatment is pemetrexed (Alimta). This drug acts by suppressing three different enzymes that are required to feed the cancer cell and has been described by as a "revved-up" version of methotrexate. It is currently approved in the United States for use in other cancer types and is under investigation in breast cancer.

TARGETED (BIOLOGIC) THERAPY: *Targeted* or *biologic therapy* refers to a medication or drug that targets a specific pathway in the growth and development of a tumor. By attacking or blocking these important targets, the therapy helps to fight the tumor itself. The targets themselves are typically various molecules (or small particles) in the body that are known or suspected to play a role in cancer formation.

HER-2 TARGETED THERAPY: The presence of the growth factor HER-2 on the surface of breast cancer cells, seen in 25 percent of breast cancers, is associated with more aggressive cancers. Trastuzumab (Herceptin) is a drug used to treat breast cancers that overexpress HER-2. It is a monoclonal antibody that works by binding to the HER-2 receptors on the surface of the cell and suppressing excess growth. Herceptin was approved in 1998 for the treatment of women with HER-2-positive metastatic breast cancer. In 2005, four large, randomized clinical trials showed a substantial benefit from adding Herceptin to standard chemotherapy in early stage, HER-2-positive breast cancer patients. Breast cancer recurrences were reduced by 50 percent, and deaths were reduced by 25 percent. These findings represented a very significant advance in breast cancer treatment.

Several other drugs that target the HER-2 protein are in clinical development. Lapatinib (Tykerb) is an oral agent that targets not just HER-2 but also its relative, HER-1 (also known as epidermal growth factor receptor, or EGFR). Tykerb has shown promise in early clinical trials, even in patients whose cancers are progressing on Herceptin. Large Phase III trials in metastatic breast cancer are ongoing, and studies in earlier stages of breast cancer are in the planning stages.

ANTI-ANGIOGENESIS AGENTS: In order for cancer to grow, blood vessels must be formed to feed the cancer cells. This process of blood vessel growth is called angiogenesis. Cancer cells secrete substances that stimulate the development of new blood vessels. Researchers are studying ways of halting this blood vessel development with drugs called angiogenesis inhibitors, in the hope that they will prevent cancers from growing and spreading.

Bevacizumab (Avastin) is a monoclonal antibody that binds to an important protein called vascular endothelial growth factor (VEGF). VEGF is responsible for new blood vessel growth in cancerous tumors. Avastin works by blocking the growth of these new blood vessels, which carry food and oxygen to the tumor, essentially choking the blood supply to the tumor and causing it to die. By doing this, Avastin helps chemotherapy drugs kill more cancer cells.

Avastin is approved for treating advanced colorectal cancer and also has proven efficacy in lung cancer. It may also have a role in the treatment of breast cancer. A recent clinical trial showed that adding Avastin to the chemotherapy drug Taxol nearly doubled the time it took for cancer to grow in women with metastatic breast cancer, compared with women who received Taxol alone. Many additional clinical trials of Avastin in both early stage and metastatic breast cancer are ongoing. Several other promising angiogenesis inhibitors are in clinical development, including some that can be taken orally.

BISPHOSPHONATES: Bisphosphonates are a class of drugs most commonly used to prevent and treat osteoporosis, since their main action is to prevent bone breakdown. When bisphosphonates are added to chemotherapy or endocrine therapy in patients with bone involvement from breast cancer, they can reduce pain, fractures and other complications of bone metastases.

Pamidronate (Aredia) and zoledronic acid (Zometa) are the bisphosphonates currently available in the United States for the treatment of bone metastases. Ibandronate (Bondronat, Boniva) and clodronate (Bonefos) are bisphosphonates available in oral form that are approved in other parts of the world for the treatment of bone metastases, and which are under investigation in the United States. A recently opened trial by the Southwest Oncology Group (SWOG S0308) is comparing intravenous Zometa to oral Bondronat in breast cancer patients with newly detected bone metastases.

There are encouraging early studies from Europe suggesting that bisphosphonates given at high doses to early stage breast cancer patients at the time of diagnosis may actually be able to prevent the spread of breast cancer to the bone and decrease deaths due to breast cancer. An ongoing clinical trial (SWOG S0307) is comparing several of these bisphosphonates in the early stage breast cancer setting, with the hope of preventing bone metastases from occurring.

OTHER PROMISING BIOLOGICALLY TARGETED AGENTS: Targeted therapies that show promise in breast cancer (but are not yet FDA-approved) include RAD001 (everolimus), an inhibitor of the mTOR protein, which is a key protein involved in regulating cell survival and growth.

Tipifarnib (Zarnestra) is a targeted therapy in the class called farnesyl transferase inhibitors. This drug stops proteins that promote the growth of breast cancer cells. It is under investigation in clinical trials in combination with endocrine therapies as well as chemotherapy drugs.

Sunitinib malate (Sutent) is a drug with multiple targets that include blood vessel growth (angiogenesis) as well as cell growth and survival pathways. It was approved in 2006 for certain gastrointestinal and kidney cancer patients. Encouraging early results have also been reported in breast cancer, and several trials of this drug are ongoing in advanced disease.

Laboratory studies suggest that the insulin-like growth factor receptor (IGFR) pathway may be another important target for breast cancer therapy. A monoclonal antibody targeting IGFR (IMC-A12) is currently in very early stages of testing in cancer patients whose cancers resist more conventional treatments.

Several versions of cancer vaccines, using a variety of targets and strategies, are also under investigation in breast cancer. There are literally hundreds more exciting targets and compounds being studied in the laboratory and in early stage clinical trials in breast cancer patients. Some of these agents will undoubtedly prove to be ineffective in breast cancer, or possibly too toxic, but there is a high probability that at least a few of them will someday soon be available to help improve survival and prevent recurrences of breast cancer.

Survivorship

Over 2 million breast cancer survivors are alive in the United States today, and these numbers continue to increase. The end of cancer treatment is not the end of the cancer experience. Life after cancer treatment brings diverse and sometimes unexpected challenges. The past decade has brought about an increased interest in studying the physical and emotional issues that affect breast cancer survivors. The National Cancer Institute's Office of Cancer Survivorship (http://cancercontrol.cancer.gov/ocs/) was created in 1996 to study the effect of cancer and its treatment and to enhance the length and quality of life in cancer survivors.

Research is ongoing to develop strategies that breast cancer survivors can adopt after the end of their treatment to decrease their risk of a cancer recurrence and improve their quality of life. Ongoing clinical trials are evaluating both conventional and complementary/alternative approaches to managing menopausal symptoms, including hot flashes and vaginal dryness. Other studies are looking at ways to treat the fatigue and cognitive problems experienced by some breast cancer survivors for months to years after the end of their treatment.

Important recent trials have shown that lifestyle strategies can reduce the risk of a breast cancer recurrence. The Women's Intervention Nutrition Study (WINS) examined the effect of a low-fat diet on postmenopausal women with early stage breast cancer. It showed that the risk of breast cancer recurrence was 24 percent lower for the women on a low-fat diet. Another recent study showed that regular exercise may significantly reduce the risk of breast cancer recurrence. Women with breast cancer who walked or did other types of moderate exercise for three to five hours per week were 50 percent less likely to die from the disease than sedentary women. There were tremendous additional benefits to overall health that came from adopting a healthy diet and increasing physical activity.

Looking Forward

Breast cancer, the most frequently diagnosed cancer in American women, is a complex and devastating disease. Thanks to exciting research advancements in the past decade, we have achieved a better understanding of breast cancer. As a result, we have made strides toward improving breast cancer prevention, diagnosis and treatment strategies. Although the future is promising, we have a long way to go before we are able to eradicate breast cancer in this country. The surest way to achieve success in our quest for a cure is to foster and ensure funding for broad-ranging research, from basic laboratory work at the cellular level to clinical trials in breast cancer patients.

"I Will Survive"

CHAPTER 21

Advocacy: Getting Involved, Making a Difference

When the timing is right and breast cancer survivors have regained their strength and energy, they may seek involvement in cancer-related awareness and advocacy activities. Getting involved can be especially empowering for individuals, helping them to feel more positive about their own personal experience while making a difference for those who will follow in their footsteps.

Volunteer Activities

Volunteers are powerful advocates and ambassadors for organizations in the community. When choosing an organization to volunteer for, become familiar with the mission, programs and services provided so that you select an agency that is aligned with your beliefs and values.

WAYS TO GET INVOLVED:

- Contact the volunteer services department at one of your local hospitals or cancer centers.
- Contact the volunteer coordinator at a cancer support group in your area to help others who are experiencing cancer.
- Contact a cancer-related organization in your area to increase breast cancer awareness or help with a cancer awareness/education event during October, Breast Cancer Awareness Month.
- Get involved and get healthy at the same time by taking part in local "fun" runs or walks that support breast cancer programs. For

example, the Puget Sound Affiliate of Susan G. Komen for the Cure organizes the annual Race for the Cure®. All people, regardless of age or physical skill, can participate, and the race features a tribute to breast cancer survivors.

Political Advocacy

National organizations and campaigns are always seeking "strong voices"— survivors, family members and friends—who are willing to speak about their experiences and share their opinions and concerns. It is not necessary to be a scientist or doctor; some of the best advocates speak from their hearts.

SUSAN G. KOMEN FOR THE CURE: The Komen foundation has a rich history in public policy advocacy that spans more than twenty years. To achieve its mission of eradicating breast cancer as a life-threatening disease by advancing research, education, screening and treatment, the foundation believes that scientific progress must be complemented by sound public policy. In this regard, the foundation works to influence policy makers at the federal, state and local levels to increase public investment in quality breast health care and breast cancer care.

As part of its advocacy efforts, the foundation has established Komen Champions for the Cure, a structured grassroots program designed to educate Congress, the president and other policy makers about breast cancer through community involvement.

An important component of Komen Champions for the Cure is the interactive website, www.ActNowEndBreastCancer.org. This virtual advocacy forum offers every American the opportunity to influence the federal government on crucial breast cancer issues by contacting their members of Congress. Anyone can take action and become a Komen e-Champion. United, we can make a difference in the fight against breast cancer.

THE NATIONAL BREAST CANCER COALITION (NBCC): NBCC unites breast cancer advocates across the nation in a grassroots effort to influence public policy to increase funding for breast cancer research and to foster laws and policies supporting the fight against breast cancer. The NBCC has made great strides in creating opportunities for breast cancer survivors to influence and offer input into research, clinical trials and national policy.

෴

The firsthand experiences of breast cancer patients and survivors are crucial in informing policy makers about local needs that affect real people. By becoming involved in advocacy you can increase public investment in breast health and breast cancer care by educating Congress, the president, and other policy makers on issues important to women and families facing breast cancer.

"Stronger Together"

❦

Western Washington Breast Cancer Treatment Centers

I n addition to these treatment centers, please also see Appendix B, Organizations and Resources.

ABERDEEN

GRAYS HARBOR COMMUNITY HOSPITAL
915 Anderson Drive
Aberdeen, WA 98520
(360) 537-5000
www.ghchwa.org

WESTERN WASHINGTON ONCOLOGY
954 Anderson Drive, #102
Aberdeen, WA 98520
(360) 533-6906
www.wwctc.com

ANACORTES

ISLAND HOSPITAL
Cancer Care Center
1211 24th Street
Anacortes, WA 98221-2590
(360) 299-1300, ext. 4200
www.islandhospital.org

ARLINGTON

CASCADE VALLEY HOSPITAL AND CLINIC
330 S Stillaguamish Avenue
Arlington, WA 98223-1642
(360) 435-2133
www.cascadevalley.org

AUBURN

AUBURN REGIONAL CENTER FOR CANCER CARE
222 2nd Street NE
Auburn, WA 98002
(253) 333-2737
www.auburncancercare.com

AUBURN REGIONAL MEDICAL CENTER
Plaza One, 202 N Division Street
Auburn, WA 98001
(253) 833-7711
www.armcuhs.com

BREAST DIAGNOSTIC CENTER
721 M Street NE, #100
Auburn, WA 98002
(253) 735-1991
www.breastdiagnostic.com

RAINIER ONCOLOGY
222 2nd Street NE, Suite B
Auburn, WA 98002
(253) 887-9333
www.rainieroncology.com

BELLEVUE

OVERLAKE HOSPITAL
Breast Health Center
1135 116th Avenue NE
Bellevue, WA 98004
(425) 688-5985
Cancer Resource Center, (425) 688-5986
www.overlakehospital.org

BELLINGHAM

ST. JOSEPH HOSPITAL COMMUNITY CANCER CENTER
3217 Squalicum Parkway
Bellingham, WA 98225
(360) 738-6706
www.peacehealth.org

BREMERTON

HARRISON MEMORIAL HOSPITAL
2520 Cherry Avenue
Bremerton, WA 98310
(800) 281-4024, (360) 377-3911
Harrison Radiation Oncology, (360) 475-8545
Inpatient Oncology Unit, (360) 792-6880
www.harrisonhospital.org

OLYMPIC HEMATOLOGY AND ONCOLOGY
2770 Clare Avenue, #A
Bremerton, WA 98310
(360) 479-6154
www.olympiconcology.com

BURIEN

HIGHLINE HOSPITAL CANCER CARE
16251 Sylvester Road SW
Seattle, WA 98166
(206) 439-5577
www.highlinehospital.org

COUPEVILLE

WHIDBEY GENERAL HOSPITAL
Community Cancer Center
101 N Main
Coupeville, WA 98239
(360) 678-7624
www.whidbeygeneral.org

COVINGTON

MULTICARE REGIONAL CANCER CENTER-COVINGTON MULTICARE CLINIC
17700 SE 272nd, Suite 300
Covington WA 98042
Medical Oncology, (253) 372-7060
www.multicare.org
Inpatient facilities: Tacoma General and Allenmore hospitals

PUGET SOUND CANCER CENTERS
21605 76th Avenue W, Suite 200
Edmonds, WA 98026
(425) 775-1677
www.pscc.cc
Inpatient facility: Stevens Hospital

STEVENS HOSPITAL
Oncology Center
Swedish Institute at Stevens Hospital Puget Sound Cancer Centers
21601 76th Avenue W
Edmonds, WA 98026
Hospital main line, (425) 640-4000
www.stevenshealthcare.org

THE EVERETT CLINIC
Center for Cancer Care
4005 Hoyt Avenue
Everett, WA 98201
(425) 339-5433
www.everettclinic.com
Inpatient facility: Providence Everett Medical Center

GROUP HEALTH COOPERATIVE
Everett Medical Center
Breast Center
2930 Maple Street
Everett, WA 98201
(800) 422-2844, (425) 261-1541
www.ghc.org

PROVIDENCE EVERETT MEDICAL CENTER
Cancer Program
916 Pacific Avenue
Everett, WA 98206
(425) 258-7255
www.providence.org
Providence Everett Medical Center
Comprehensive Breast Center
900 Pacific Avenue
Everett, WA 98201
(425) 258-7900
www.providence.org

WESTERN WASHINGTON MEDICAL GROUP
Oncology
3226 Nassau
Everett, WA 98201
(425) 258-9388
www.wwmedgroup.com
Inpatient facility: Providence Everett Medical Center

FEDERAL WAY

BREAST DIAGNOSTIC CENTER
700 S 320th
Federal Way, WA 98003
(253) 839-8779
www.breastdiagnostic.com

FRANCISCAN CANCER CENTER
Cancer Care at St. Francis Hospital
34515 9th Avenue S
Federal Way, WA 98003
(253) 944-8100
www.fhshealth.org

FORKS

FORKS COMMUNITY HOSPITAL
530 Bogachiel Way
Forks, WA 98331
(360) 374-6271
www.forkshospital.org

GIG HARBOR

**MULTICARE REGIONAL CANCER CENTER-
GIG HARBOR MULTICARE CLINIC**
4700 Point Fosdick Drive
Gig Harbor, WA 98335
Medical Oncology, (253) 851-2328
www.multicare.org
Inpatient facilities: Tacoma General and Allenmore hospitals

ILWACO

OCEAN BEACH HOSPITAL
PO Drawer H
Ilwaco, WA 98624
(360) 642-3181
www.oceanbeachhospital.org

KIRKLAND

CASCADE CANCER CENTER
12303 NE 130th Lane, Suite 120
Kirkland, WA 98034-3041
(425) 899-3181
www.evergreenhealthcare.org
Inpatient facility: Evergreen Hospital

LAKEWOOD

FRANCISCAN CANCER CENTER
St. Clare Hospital
Outpatient Cancer Center
11315 Bridgeport Way SW
Lakewood, WA 98499
(253) 588-1711
www.fhshealth.org

LONGVIEW

ST. JOHN MEDICAL CENTER
Peace Health Medical Group
Cancer Care Center
1615 Delaware Street
Longview, WA 98632
(360) 414-2000
www.peacehealth.org

ST. JOHN MEDICAL CENTER
Peace Health Women's Pavilion
1660 Delaware Street
Longview, WA 98362
(360) 414-2800
www.peacehealth.org

HEALTH SOUTH CLINIC
Lymphedema Treatment
Debra Hadler, PT
900 Fir Street
Longview, WA 98632
(360) 748-1580
The only lymphedema treatment option in this area

MONROE

VALLEY GENERAL HOSPITAL
Snohomish County Public Hospital Dist. No. 1
14701 179th SE
PO Box 646
Monroe, WA 98272
(360) 794-7497
www.valleygeneral.com

MOUNT VERNON

SKAGIT DIGITAL IMAGING LLC
DBA Breast Care Center
1320 E Division Street
Mount Vernon, WA 98274
(888) 371-2812, (360) 424-9607

SKAGIT VALLEY HOSPITAL CANCER CARE CENTER, WITH THE SEATTLE CANCER CARE ALLIANCE
1415 E Kincaid Street
Mount Vernon, WA 98274
(360) 424-4111
www.skagitvalleyhospital.org

OLYMPIA/LACEY

CAPITAL MEDICAL CENTER
3900 Capital Mall Drive SW
Olympia, WA 98502
(360) 754-5858
www.capitalmedical.com

GROUP HEALTH COOPERATIVE
Olympia Medical Center
700 Lilly Road NE
Olympia, WA 98506
(800) 565-1393, ext. 7645, (360) 923-7645
www.ghc.org

PROVIDENCE AT ST. PETER HOSPITAL
413 Lilly Road NE
Olympia, WA 98506-5166
(888) 492-9480, (360) 493-7768
Oncology Unit, (360) 943-7903
www.providence.org

RADIANT CARE
Radiation Oncology
Western Washington Cancer Center Building
4525 3rd Avenue SE, Suite 100
Lacey, WA 98503
(360) 412-8960

WESTERN WASHINGTON ONCOLOGY
Western Washington Cancer Center Building
4525 3rd Avenue SE, Suite 200
Lacey, WA 98503
(360) 754-3934
www.wwctc.com

PORT ANGELES

OLYMPIC MEDICAL CENTER
939 Caroline Street
Port Angeles, WA 98362
(360) 417-7000
www.olympicmedical.org

OLYMPIC MEDICAL IMAGING
1102 E Front Street
Port Angeles, WA 98362
(360) 565-9000
www.olympicmedical.org

PORT TOWNSEND

JEFFERSON HEALTHCARE
834 Sheridan
Port Townsend, WA 98368
(360) 385-2200
www.jeffersonhealthcare.org

POULSBO

INHEALTH IMAGING
20700 Bond Road NE
Poulsbo, WA 98370
(360) 598-3141

PUYALLUP

GOOD SAMARITAN CANCER CENTER
400 15th Avenue SE
Puyallup, WA 98372
(253) 697-HOPE (4673)
Puget Sound Regional Breast Cancer Center at Good Samaritan, (253) 697-4862
www.goodsamhealth.org

GOOD SAMARITAN HOSPITAL
407 14th Avenue SE
Puyallup, WA 98372
(253) 697-4000
www.goodsamhealth.org

MEDICAL IMAGING NORTHWEST
222 15th Avenue SE and 11212 Sunrise Boulevard E, Suite 200
Puyallup, WA 98372
(253) 841-4353
www.minw.com

REDMOND

GROUP HEALTH COOPERATIVE
Eastside Hospital, Breast Center
2700 152nd Avenue NE
Redmond, WA 98052
(800) 995-5658, ext. 5723, (425) 883-5723
www.ghc.org

RENTON

VALLEY BREAST CENTER AT VALLEY MEDICAL CENTER
4003 Talbot Road S, Suite 470
Renton, WA 98058
(425) 656-5588
www.valleymed.org

BREAST DIAGNOSTIC CENTER-SOUTHCENTER
Southcenter Professional Plaza
411 Strander Boulevard, #303
Seattle, WA 98188
(206) 575-9123
www.breastdiagnostic.com

GROUP HEALTH COOPERATIVE
Capitol Hill Campus, Main Building
201 16th Avenue E
Seattle, WA 98112
(800) 562-6300, ext. 3939, (206) 326-3939
www.ghc.org

HARBORVIEW MEDICAL CENTER
Breast Clinic, with the Seattle Cancer Care Alliance
325 9th Avenue
Seattle, WA 98104
(206) 731-8597
www.uwmedicine.org

PACIFIC MEDICAL CENTERS
Madison Oncology
1101 Madison Street, Suite 301
Seattle, WA 98104
(206) 505-1101
www.pacmed.org
Inpatient facilities: Virginia Mason Hospital and Swedish Medical Center

THE POLYCLINIC
1145 Broadway
Seattle, WA 98122
(206) 329-1760
www.polyclinic.com
Inpatient facility: Swedish Medical Center

PUGET SOUND CANCER CENTERS
1560 N 115th Street, G-16
Seattle, WA 98133
(206) 365-8252
www.pscc.cc
Inpatient facility: Northwest Hospital

SEATTLE BREAST CENTER AT NORTHWEST HOSPITAL
1560 N 115th, Suite 104
Seattle, WA 98133
(206) 368-1749
www.seattlebreastcenter.org
Hospital main line, (206) 364-0500
www.nwhospital.org
Inpatient facility: Northwest Hospital

SEATTLE CANCER CARE ALLIANCE (SCCA)
Women's Center for Breast and Gynecologic Cancer
825 Eastlake Avenue E
Seattle, WA 98109
Appointments: (206) 288-7400
(800) 804-8824
www.seattlecca.org

SEATTLE CANCER TREATMENT AND WELLNESS CENTER
122 16th Avenue E
Seattle, WA 98112
(800) 321-9272, (888) 321-9272, (206) 292-9272
www.cancercenter.com

SWEDISH CANCER INSTITUTE AT HIGHLINE COMMUNITY HOSPITAL
16251 Sylvester Road SW
Seattle, WA 98166
(206) 386-2626
www.hchnet.org

SWEDISH MEDICAL CENTER
Swedish Cancer Institute
Breast Care Center
First Hill Campus
1101 Madison Street, Suite 310
Seattle, WA 98104
(206) 386-3776
www.swedish.org

SWEDISH COMPREHENSIVE BREAST CENTER
Providence Campus
1600 E Jefferson Street, Suite 300
Seattle, WA 98122
(206) 320-4800
www.swedish.org

SWEDISH WOMEN'S DIAGNOSTIC IMAGING CENTER
First Hill Campus

1221 Madison Street, Suite 520
Seattle, WA 98104
(206) 215-3939
www.swedish.org

SWEDISH WOMEN'S IMAGING CENTER
Ballard Campus
5300 Tallman Avenue NW, 2nd Floor, Women's Imaging
Seattle, WA 98107
(206) 781-6349
www.swedish.org

UNIVERSITY OF WASHINGTON MEDICAL CENTER
Seattle Cancer Care Alliance
1959 NE Pacific Street
Seattle, WA 98195
(206) 598-4100
www.uwmedicine.org

VIRGINIA MASON MEDICAL CENTER
The Floyd and Delores Jones Cancer Institute at Virginia Mason
1100 9th Avenue
Seattle, WA 98101
Appointments: (800) 354-9527 (in state), (206) 223-6600
(800) 356-0017 (out of state)
www.virginiamason.org

SEDRO-WOOLLEY

UNITED GENERAL HOSPITAL
North Puget Oncology
2000 Hospital Drive
Sedro-Woolley, WA 98284
Breast Center, (360) 424-9607
North Puget Oncology, (360) 856-7588
www.unitedgeneral.org

SEQUIM

OLYMPIC MEDICAL CANCER CENTER, WITH THE SEATTLE CANCER CARE ALLIANCE
844 N 5th Avenue
Sequim, WA 98382
(360) 683-9895
www.olympicmedical.org

OLYMPIC MEDICAL IMAGING
777 N 5th Avenue
Sequim, WA 98382
(360) 582-2620
www.olympicmedical.org
Inpatient facility: Olympic Medical Center

SHELTON

MASON GENERAL HOSPITAL
Oncology
901 Mt. View Drive, Building #1
Shelton, WA 98584
(360) 426-1611
www.masongeneral.com

SILVERDALE

GROUP HEALTH COOPERATIVE
Silverdale Medical Center
10452 Silverdale Way NW
Silverdale, WA 98383
(800) 645-6605, ext. 7555, (360) 307-7555
www.ghc.org

WOMEN'S DIAGNOSTIC CENTER, A DIVISION
OF ADVANCED MEDICAL IMAGING
1780 NW Myhre, #1220
Silverdale, WA 98383
(800) 972-9264, (360) 337-6550
www.amiradiology.com

TACOMA

FRANCISCAN CANCER CENTER
St. Joseph Medical Center
Outpatient Cancer Center
1717 South J Street
Tacoma, WA 98405
(253) 426-4101
www.fhshealth.org
Group Health Cooperative

TACOMA MEDICAL CENTER
209 Martin Luther King Jr. Way
Tacoma, WA 98405
(800) 858-9996, ext. 3480, (253) 596-3480
www.ghc.org

MADIGAN ARMY MEDICAL CENTER AT FORT LEWIS
Oncology Clinic
Building 9040, Fitzsimmons Drive
Tacoma, WA 98431
(253) 968-0975 or (253) 968-1111
www.mamc.amedd.army.mil/mamc/mamcexthome.htm
Inpatient facility: Madigan Army Medical Center

MULTICARE REGIONAL CANCER CENTER-ALLENMORE HOSPITAL
1901 S Union Avenue, Suite A-240
Tacoma, WA 98405
Medical Oncology, (253) 459-6640
www.multicare.org

MULTICARE REGIONAL CANCER CENTER-TACOMA GENERAL HOSPITAL
315 Martin Luther King Jr. Way
Tacoma, WA 98405
Medical Oncology, (253) 403-1677
Radiation Oncology, (253) 403-4994
Inpatient Unit, (253) 403-1070
www.multicare.org

VANCOUVER

SOUTHWEST WASHINGTON MEDICAL CENTER
Breast Care Center
200 NE Mother Joseph Place, Suite 240
Vancouver, WA 98664
(360) 514-6161
www.swmedicalcenter.com

Puget Sound Cancer Centers:
Quick Reference Chart

** pending

Auburn Regional Center for Cancer Care (Auburn)
Auburn Regional Medical Center (Auburn)
Breast Diagnostic Center (Auburn, Federal Way, Southcenter)
Capital Medical Center (Olympia)
Cascade Cancer Center at Evergreen Hospital (Kirkland)
Cascade Valley Hospital & Clinic (Arlington)
The Everett Clinic, Center for Cancer Care (Everett)
Forks Community Hospital (Forks)
Franciscan Cancer Center, Cancer Care at St. Francis Hospital (Federal Way)
Franciscan Cancer Center, St. Clare Hospital (Lakewood)
Franciscan Cancer Center, St. Joseph Medical Center (Tacoma)
Good Samaritan Cancer Center & Puget Sound Regional Breast Cancer Center (Puyallup)
Good Samaritan Hospital (Puyallup)
Grays Harbor Community Hospital (Aberdeen)
Group Health Cooperative (6 locations)
Harborview Medical Center (Seattle)
Harrison Memorial Hospital (Bremerton)
Health South Clinic (Longview)
Highline Cancer Center (Burien)
InHealth Imaging (Poulsbo)
Island Hospital (Anacortes)
Jefferson Healthcare (Port Townsend)
Madigan Army Medical Center (Tacoma)
Mason General Hospital (Shelton)
Medical Imaging North West (Puyallup)
MultiCare Regional Cancer Care (Covington, Gig Harbor, Tacoma)
Seattle Breast Center at Northwest Hospital (Seattle)
Ocean Beach Hospital (Ilwaco)
Olympic Hematology & Oncology (Bremerton)
Olympic Medical Cancer Center (Sequim)
Olympic Medical Center (Port Angeles)
Olympic Medical Imaging (Sequim)

DIAGNOSTIC				TREATMENT						SERVICES						INFO	
Diagnostic Biopsy	Mammography	Ultrasound	Breast MRI	Breast Surgery	Medical Oncology	Chemotherapy	Radiation Therapy	Reconstruction	Clinical Trials	Financial Counseling	Lymphedema Treatment	Physical Therapy	Nutrition Counseling	Social Services	Support Group	Cancer Education	Genetics Counseling
							X		X							X	
X	X	X		X	X		X			X	X	X	X	X			
X	X	X								X							
X	X	X		X		X	X	X		X	X	X	X	X		X	X
X	X	X	X	X	X	X	X	X	X	X	X		X	X	X	X	X
	X	X		X	X	X				X			X	X		X	
X	X	X	X	X	X	X							X				
X	X	X			X	X						X		X			
X	X	X		X	X	X	X	X	X	X	X	X	X	X	X	X	
X	X	X		X	X	X			X	X		X	X	X		X	
X	X	X		X	X	X	X	X	X	X	X	X	X	X		X	
X				X	X	X			X	X		X	X	X	X	X	X
X		X		X	X	X			X	X	X	X	X	X	X	X	
X	X	X	X	X		X				X	X	X	X	X		X	
X	X	X	X	X	X	X	X	X	X	X	X	X	X	X	X	X	X
X	X	X	X	X	X	X	X	X	X	X	X	X	X	X	X	X	X
X	X	X	X	X	X	X	X	X	X	X	X	X	X	X	X	X	X
											X	X					
X	X	X	X	X	X	X	X	X	X	X	X	X	X	X	X	X	X
X	X	X	X														
X	X	X	X	X	X	X			X	X	X	X	X	X	X	X	
X	X	X		X						X	X	X	X	X	X	X	
X	X	X	**	X	X	X	X	X	X	X		X	X	X	X	X	X
X	X	X		X						X	X	X	X	X	X		
X	X	X	X														
X	X	X	X	X	X	X	X	X	X	X	X	X	X	X	X	X	X
X	X	X	X	X	X	X	X	X	X	X	X	X	X	X	X	X	X
X	X	X	X	X	X	X				X			X	X		X	
				X	X				X	X	X		X				X
				X	X	X			X				X	X		X	
X	X	X		X	X	X	X	X		X	X	X	X	X		X	
	X	X															

Puget Sound Cancer Centers: Quick Reference Chart

** pending

Olympic Medical Imaging (Port Angeles)

Overlake Hospital (Bellevue)

Pacific Medical Centers (several locations, Seattle area)

The Polyclinic (Seattle)

Providence Everett Medical Center, Comprehensive Breast Cancer Center (Everett)

Providence Everett Medical Center, Cancer Program (Everett)

Providence at St. Peter Hospital (Olympia)

Puget Sound Cancer Centers (Edmonds, Seattle)

Radiant Care (Lacey)

Rainier Oncology (Auburn)

Seattle Cancer Care Alliance (UWMC) (Seattle)

Seattle Cancer Treatment and Wellness Center (Seattle)

Skagit Digital Imaging LLC, DBA Breast Care Center (Mount Vernon)

Skagit Valley Hospital Cancer Care Center (Mount Vernon)

St. John Medical Center, Peace Health Medical Group & Women's Pavilion (Longview)

St. Joseph Hospital Community Cancer Program (Bellingham)

Stevens Hospital, Oncology Center (Edmonds)

Southwest Washington Medical Center (Vancouver)

Swedish Cancer Institute at Highline Community Hospital (Burien)

Swedish Medical Center (several locations, Seattle area)

United General Hospital, North Puget Oncology (Sedro Woolley)

UW Medical Center (SCCA) (Seattle)

Valley Breast Center at Valley Medical Center (Renton)

Valley General Hospital (Monroe)

Virginia Mason Medical Center (Seattle)

Western Washington Medical Group (Everett)

Western Washington Oncology (Aberdeen)

Western Washington Oncology (Lacey)

Whidbey General Hospital, Community Cancer Center (Coupeville)

Women's Diagnostic Center (Silverdale)

	DIAGNOSTIC			TREATMENT						SERVICES						INFO	
Diagnostic Biopsy	Mammography	Ultrasound	Breast MRI	Breast Surgery	Medical Oncology	Chemotherapy	Radiation Therapy	Reconstruction	Clinical Trials	Financial Counseling	Lymphedema Treatment	Physical Therapy	Nutrition Counseling	Social Services	Support Group	Cancer Education	Genetics Counseling
X	X																
X	X	X	**	X	X	X	X	X	X	X	X	X	X	X	X	X	X
X				X	X	X	X			X	X	X	X	X	X	X	X
X	X	X	X	X	X	X			X	X	X				X	X	
X	X	X	X						X	X		X	X	X	X	X	X
X	X	X	X	X	X	X	X	X	X	X	X	X	X	X	X	X	X
X	X	X	X	X	X	X	X	X	X	X	X	X	X	X	X	X	X
X	X	X	X	X	X	X			X	X	X	X	X	X	X	X	X
							X									X	
					X	X			X	X				X			
X	X	X	X	X	X	X	X	X	X	X	X	X	X	X	X	X	X
					X	X				X			X	X	X	X	
X	X	X															
X	X	X	X	X	X	X	X	X	X	X	X		X	X	X	X	
X	X	X	X	X	X	X	X	X	X	X		X	X	X	X	X	X
							X		X	X			X	X	X	X	
X	X	X		X	X	X	X	X		X			X	X	X	X	
X	X	X	X	X	X	X	X	X	X	X	X	X	X	X	X	X	X
							X								X	X	
X	X	X	X	X	X	X	X	X	X	X	X	X	X	X	X	X	X
X	X	X	X		X	X	X			X	X	X	X	X	X	X	X
X	X	X	X	X	X	X	X	X	X	X	X	X	X	X	X	X	
X	X	X		X	X	X				X			X	X			
X	X	X	X	X	X	X	X	X	X	X	X	X	X	X	X	X	X
					X	X			X	X						X	
					X	X			X								
X				X	X	X			X	X						X	
X	X	X		X	X	X		X	X	X	X	X	X	X	X	X	
X	X	X															

I was worried about a very small, soft, pea-sized lump in my breast when I first went to visit my doctor and, at the same time, was wondering if I was pregnant. My doctor told me I *was* pregnant (good news) and that the lump I felt was nothing to worry about. So I didn't, happy to be pregnant. After giving birth and nursing for one year and six months, I started checking my breasts for lumps and in the same quadrant as before, I found five rock-hard lumps and realized it was uncomfortable to lay on my stomach. I was diagnosed with stage II cancer.

My life changed dramatically: I changed my job and I reached out for support with regard to domestic violence. I later divorced and now am a single mother. I didn't know how strong I was, and what a team my daughter and I alone could make. I remember my mother was a single mom dealing with life-changing disabilities. I am lucky I am not disabled; I have survived cancer. My daughter accompanied me at my chemotherapy appointments at only three-years old. She cried when I needed to shave my head—I explained that my head hurt because my hair felt like needles poking at it—and then she realized it was okay to shave your head. She knows what cancer is, how to lead a healthy life and that she can count on Mami to ensure that our home is maintained as sacred.

—*Michelle Di Miscio, Breast Cancer Survivor*

Organizations and Resources

D iscovering that you have breast cancer can be a very lonely experience until you realize that many resources, organizations and information sources exist to help you. From national hotlines to local transportation assistance to personal accounts of the breast cancer journey, Appendixes B and C contain organizations, resources and publications you may find helpful.

Organizations and Resources—General

Local Organizations and Resources—General

AMERICAN CANCER SOCIETY (ACS)
Publications, information and emotional support. Information on pharmaceutical company drug financial assistance programs. ACS programs differ geographically, but may include I Can Cope (education), Reach to Recovery (emotional and practical support; brochures available in various languages on breast cancer early detection, breast self-exam and diagnosis, call 800-227-2345), Spanish-language translation and visitation services (800-729-5588 or 425-741-8949), Road to Recovery (transportation assistance), and Look Good . . . Feel Better (grooming and appearance during treatment). Patient services programs may include transportation, reimbursement and housing. Access the Cancer Survivors Network using the ACS website. www.cancer.org.
Everett office, 728 134th Street SW, Suite 101, Everett, WA 98204, (800) 729-5588, (425) 741-8949.
Great West Division office, 2120 1st N, Seattle, WA 98109, (800) 729-1151, (206) 283-1152
National information line, (800) ACS-2345

ANGEL CARE BREAST CANCER FOUNDATION
Provides caring support by breast cancer survivors helping to empower the newly diagnosed. (425) 861-5655, www.angelcarefoundation.org.

BREAST CANCER FUND
Identifies and advocates for elimination of environmental and other preventable causes of breast cancer. PO Box 15145, Seattle, WA 98115, (206) 524-4405; 1388 Sutter Street, Suite 400, San Francisco, CA 94019-5400, (415) 346-8223, www. breastcancerfund.org.

BREAST CANCER RESOURCE CENTER
Provides referral and educational information through Quiet Voices, a program providing surgeons' offices with gift bags containing breast cancer literature and a list of local resources for newly diagnosed patients. 3502 S 12th Street, Suite A, Tacoma, WA 98405, (253) 752-4222, www.bcrcwa.org.

CANCER LIFELINE
Provides emotional support and information about cancer-related issues. Programs include family support programs, workplace consultation, kids/parents groups, movement awareness, relaxation and stress reduction services, pain management, nutrition classes, lymphedema education and support groups. www.cancerlifeline.org. *Hotline*, (800) 255-5505, (206) 297-2500 (in King County) *Eastside campus*, 15355 SE 30th Place (Eastgate Office Park), (425) 747-4367 *Seattle campus*, 6522 Fremont Avenue N, Seattle, WA 98103, (206) 297-2100

COMMUNITY RESOURCES ONLINE (CRISIS CLINIC)
Offers an array of support services available to everyone in King County. *Community Resources Online*, (800) 621-4636, (206) 461-3200; *24-hour crisis line*, (800) 244-5767, (866) 4-CRISIS or (206) 461-3222, info@crisisclinic.org, www.crisisclinic.org.

GILDA'S CLUB
National organization providing social and emotional support along with lectures, workshops, networking groups, special events and children's programs. *Gilda's Club Seattle*, 1400 Broadway, Seattle, WA 98122, (206) 709-1400, www.gildasclubseattle.org; *National organization*, (800) 445-3248, www.gildasclub.org.

NORTHWEST HOPE AND HEALING
Provides child care, counseling, transportation, meals and education to women receiving breast cancer treatment in the Puget Sound area. www.northwesthopeandhealing.org.

SUSAN G. KOMEN FOR THE CURE-PUGET SOUND AFFILIATE
An international organization with a mission to eradicate breast cancer as a life-threatening disease by advancing research, education, screening and treatment. *Puget Sound Affiliate*, 1900 N Northlake Way, Suite 135, Seattle, WA 98103, (206) 633-0303, www.komenpugetsound.org; *Breast Care Helpline*, (800) I'M AWARE (462-9273).

WASHINGTON STATE DEPARTMENT OF HEALTH, PROFESSIONAL LICENSING DIVISION
To learn of regulated health care providers in the state of Washington. 1300 SE Quince Street, Olympia WA 98504, (360) 236-4501 or (360) 236-48QO (for regulated providers).

National Organizations and Resources—General

AMERICAN BREAST CANCER FOUNDATION
Their mission is to provide a fighting chance to every life threatened by breast cancer no matter the person's age, race, sex or financial challenge. They provide mammography screening, assistance programs, do research and offer support for breast cancer patients and their families. www.abcf.org.

ASSOCIATION OF CANCER ONLINE RESOURCES
Current information about breast cancer, including patient-run websites. Click "Online Cancer Information and Support." www.acor.org.

BREAST CANCER ACTION
55 New Montgomery Street, #323, San Francisco, CA 94105, (877) 278-6722, info@bcaction.org, www.bcaction.org.

BREASTCANCER.NET
Informational articles, support, treatment and links to survivor resources. www.breastcancer.net.

BREASTCANCER.ORG
A nonprofit organization for breast cancer education. www.breastcancer.org.

CANCERCARE
Provides free professional help to people with all cancers, at all stages, through counseling, education, information and direct referral and financial assistance. 275 7th Avenue, New York, NY 10001, (800) 813-HOPE, www.cancercare.org.

CANCEREDUCATION.COM
Educational information for health care professionals, cancer patients and their family members. www.cancereducation.com.

CANCER HOPE NETWORK
Nationwide support. One-on-one emotional support for patients and families undergoing chemotherapy and/or radiation treatment from trained volunteers who have experienced the treatments themselves. 2 North Road, Suite A, Chester, NJ 07930-2308, (877) HOPENET (467-3638), www.cancerhopemetwork.org.

CANCER-RELATED LINKS
Comprehensive links to many different sites, including government and educational institution resources, cancer institutes and research centers, medical resources, journals and newsletters, disease-specific sites, alternative and complementary treatment resources and more. www.seidata.com/~marriage/rcancer.html.

CANCERSOURCE.COM
Comprehensive source of cancer information and services. www.cancersource.com.

CHEMOANGELS.COM
Support for people with cancer. www.chemoangels.com.

THE HUMOR PROJECT
A resource for humorous materials; free catalog. Holds conferences on using humor in coping with illness. 480 Broadway, Suite 210, Saratoga Springs, NY 12866, (518) 587-8770, www.humorproject.com.

IMAGINIS.COM
Comprehensive resource for information on breast cancer and women's health issues. www.imaginis.com.

LANCE ARMSTRONG FOUNDATION (LAF)
LAF believes that in your battle with cancer, knowledge is power and attitude is everything. Founded by cancer survivor and cycling champion Lance Armstrong, the LAF provides the practical information and tools that people living with cancer need to live strong. PO Box 161150, Austin, TX 78716-1150, (512) 236-8820, www.livestrong.org.

LIVING BEYOND BREAST CANCER
Information and support to live well beyond breast cancer. www.lbbc.org.

NATIONAL ASSOCIATION OF HOSPITAL HOSPITALITY HOUSES INC.
Information on lodging and support for patients and families receiving medical care away from home. PO Box 18087, Ashville, NC 28801, (800) 542-9730, helpinghomes@nahhh.org, www.hahhh.org.

NATIONAL BREAST CANCER AWARENESS MONTH
Educating women about breast cancer detection, diagnosis and treatment. www.nbcam.org.

NATIONAL BREAST CANCER COALITION (NBCC)
Active in obtaining increased funding for breast cancer research. 1101 17th Street NW, Suite 1300, Washington, DC 98036, (202) 296-7477, www.natlbcc.org.

NATIONAL CANCER INSTITUTE (NCI), CANCER INFORMATION SERVICE
Educates the public about cancer prevention, risk factors, symptoms, diagnosis, treatment and research. Information provided by phone and online (LiveHelp) by NCI Cancer Information Service information specialists. (800) 422-6237 (English and Spanish), www.cancer.gov/help.

NATIONAL CANCER SURVIVOR'S DAY FOUNDATION (NCSD)
Sponsors the celebration of life for cancer survivors, families, friends and oncology teams on the first Sunday of June in communities throughout America. PO Box 682285, Franklin, TN 37068-2285, (615) 794-3006, (615) 794-0179 (fax), www.ncsdf.org.

NATIONAL COALITION FOR CANCER SURVIVORSHIP (NCCS)

Network of groups and individuals concerned with survivorship and resources for cancer patients and their families. A clearinghouse of information and advocacy for cancer survivors. 1010 Wayne Avenue, Suite 770, Silver Spring, MD 20910, (877) 622-7937, www.canceradvocacy.org.

NATIONAL FAMILY CAREGIVERS ASSOCIATION

Membership organization dedicated to improving life for family caregivers through information, publications and education and public awareness activities. Publishes a resource guide and newsletter and matches caregivers for peer support. 10400 Connecticut Avenue, #500, Kensington, MD 20895-3944, (800) 896-3650, info@nfcacares.org, www.nfcacares.org.

NATIONAL WOMEN'S HEALTH NETWORK

Believes that with the right information, all women can make informed health decisions. Provides clear, well-researched and independent women's health information online, by mail and through a volunteer-staffed information clearinghouse. 514 10th Street NW, Suite 400, Washington, DC 20004, (202) 628-7814, nwhn@nwhn.org, www.nwhn.org.

THE NORTH AMERICAN MENOPAUSE SOCIETY

PO Box 94527, Cleveland, OH 44101, (800) 774-5342, (440) 442-7550, info@menopause.org, www.menopause.org.

ONCOLINK CANCER RESOURCE

Maintained by the University of Pennsylvania Abramson Cancer Center as an up-to-date resource on cancer. www.oncolink.org.

PEOPLE LIVING WITH CANCER

Patient-information website of the American Society of Clinical Oncology. www.plwc.org.

SHARE

Survivor-led support for women with breast or ovarian cancer, their families and friends. 1501 Broadway, Suite 704A, New York, NY 10036, (866) 891-2392, www.sharecancersupport.org.

STRANG CANCER PREVENTION CENTER

A free national resource for breast cancer risk counseling and research into breast cancer risk. 428 72nd Street, New York, NY 10021, (212) 794-4900, www.strang.org.

SUSAN LOVE, MD

The website for women, breast cancer and women's health. www.susanlovemd.org.

VITAL OPTIONS INTERNATIONAL TELESUPPORT CANCER NETWORK

Cancer communications, support and advocacy organization. www.vitaloptions.org.

THE WELLNESS COMMUNITY
International organization dedicated to providing emotional support, education and hope for people affected by cancer. 2716 Ocean Park Boulevard, Santa Monica, CA 90405, (888) 793-9355, www.thewellnesscommunity.org.

WOMEN AT RISK
A research, diagnosis and treatment group for women at high risk of developing breast cancer. Columbia-Presbyterian Medical Center, Breast Service, New York, NY 10021, (212) 305-8500, www.breastmd.org.

Y-ME
National organization for breast cancer information, support and counseling for breast cancer patients and families. 212 W Van Buren Street, Chicago, IL 60607, (800) 221-2141 (24-hour hotline, interpreters in 150 languages), (800) 986-9505 (Spanish), www.y-me.org.

Exercise, Alternative Medicine and Nontraditional Therapies

HEALTH WORLD ONLINE
An integrative approach to healing. www.healthy.net.

JOHN BASTYR UNIVERSITY
A private university with a science-based natural medicine curriculum. Offers natural health care to the community. 14500 Juanita Drive NE, Kenmore WA 98028, (425) 823-1300, www.bastyr.edu.

KNIT FOR LIFE
A network of volunteers who use the healing experience of knitting to enhance the lives of cancer patients and their caregivers during treatment and recovery. Provides a program of instruction for beginning and experienced knitters in a nontraditional therapeutic environment. All supplies provided. PO Box 31637, Seattle, WA 98103, (206) 938-9081, tanyaparieaux@earthlink.net, www.knitforlife.com.

THE LEBED METHOD
"Focus on Healing Through Movement and Dance." Range of motion exercises for breast cancer patients postsurgery. 14418 47th Place West, Lynnwood, WA 980347, (877) 365-6014, info@focusonhealing.net, www.lebedmethod.com.

NATIONAL CENTER FOR COMPLEMENTARY AND ALTERNATIVE MEDICINE (NCCAM), NATIONAL INSTITUTES OF HEALTH
NCCAM is dedicated to exploring complementary and alternative healing practices in the context of rigorous science. NCCAM Clearinghouse, PO Box 7923, Gaithersburg, MD 20898-7923, (888) 644-6226, (866) 464-3615 (TTY), info@nccam.nih.gov, http://nccam.nih.gov.

NORTHWEST INSTITUTE OF ACUPUNCTURE AND ORIENTAL MEDICINE
701 N 34th, Suite 300, Seattle, WA 98103, (206) 633-5581

OFFICE OF CANCER COMPLEMENTARY AND
ALTERNATIVE MEDICINE (OCCAM)
OCCAM was established to coordinate and enhance the activities of the National
Cancer Institute (NCI) in the arena of complementary and alternative medicine. www.
cancer.gov/cam.

OREGON COLLEGE OF ORIENTAL MEDICINE
10525 SE Cherry Blossom Drive, Portland, OR 97216, (503) 253-3443

QI GONG ASSOCIATION OF AMERICA
1220 NW Kings Boulevard, Corvallis, OR 97330, (888) 974-4664 or (541) 752-6599,
www.qi.org.

TAOIST STUDIES INSTITUTE
225 N 70th, Seattle, WA 98103, (206) 784-5632, www.taoiststudiesinstitute.org.

TEAM SURVIVOR NORTHWEST
Provides a broad range of fitness and health education programs to enable women
cancer survivors, in any stage of treatment or recovery and at any fitness level, to take
an active role in their ongoing physical and emotional healing. 200 NE Pacific Street,
#101, Seattle, WA 98105; (206) 732-8350, www.teamsurvivornw.org.

Financial, Legal and Insurance Resources

Contact your oncology social worker at your treatment center for up-to-
date resources in your area.

AMERICA'S HEALTH INSURANCE PLANS
Publishes several manuals on health and disability insurance. 601 Pennsylvania
Avenue NW, South Building, Suite 500, Washington, DC 20004, (202) 778-3200,
www.ahip.org.

DIRECTORY OF PRESCRIPTION DRUG PATIENT ASSISTANCE PROGRAMS
Provides listings of drug companies that provide prescription medicines free of charge
to physicians whose patients might not otherwise have access to necessary medicines.
(877) 477-2669, www.phrma.org.

NATIONAL COALITION FOR CANCER SURVIVORSHIP (NCCS)
Clearinghouse for information and materials on survivorship and an advocate for
cancer survivors, especially in employment, insurance and health care reform. 1010
Wayne Avenue, Suite 770, Silver Springs, MD 20910-5600, (877) 622-7937, www.
canceradvocacy.org.

NATIONAL SELF-HELP CLEARINGHOUSE

Makes referrals to regional self-help services, particularly regarding insurance concerns and employment rights. 365 5th Avenue, Suite 3300, New York, NY 10016, (212) 817-1822, info@selfhelpweb.org.

NORTHWEST JUSTICE PROJECT

Provides free civil legal services to low-income people regarding public entitlements (e.g., Medicaid and food stamps). www.nwjustice.org.
Seattle, main office, 401 2nd Avenue S, Suite 407, Seattle, WA 98104, (888) 201-1012 or (206) 464-1519, (206) 624-7501 (fax), (888) 201-9737 (TDD), njp@nwjustice.org.
Bellingham office (Whatcom, San Juan, Island, Skagit counties), 1814 Cornwall Avenue, Bellingham, WA 98225, (800) 562-8836, (360) 734-8680, (888) 201-1014 (CLEAR; client intake), (360) 734-0121 (fax), bell@nwjustice.org.
Everett office, (Snohomish County), 2731 Wetmore Avenue N, Suite 410, Everett, WA 98201, (888) 201-1017 or (425) 252-8515, (888) 201-1014 (CLEAR; client intake), (425) 252-5945 (fax), ev@nwjustice.org.
Olympia office, 711 Capitol Way S, Suite 704, Olympia, WA 98501, (888) 212-0380 or (360) 753-3610, (360) 753-0174 (fax), oly@nwjustice.org.

NORTHWEST WOMEN'S LAW CENTER

Provides legal information and referrals to private attorneys. 3161 Elliott Avenue, Suite 101, Seattle, WA 98121, (206) 621-7691 (information and referrals), (206) 682-9552 (administration), www.nwwlc.org.

SOCIAL SECURITY ADMINISTRATION

The toll-free hotline has representatives to answer questions regarding Medicare benefits. (800) 772-1213, www.ssa.gov or www.medicare.gov.

STATEWIDE HEALTH INSURANCE BENEFITS ADVISORS (SHIBA)

Washington State network of volunteers who help consumers and their families with questions about health insurance and health care access. (800) 562-6900, www.insurance.wa.gov (click on "SHIBA HelpLine").

WASHINGTON STATE BASIC HEALTH PLAN

PO Box 42683, Olympia, WA 98504-2683, (800) 660-9840, www.basichealth.hca.wa.gov.

WASHINGTON STATE DEPARTMENT OF SOCIAL AND HEALTH SERVICES

General questions, (800) 737-0617; *Customer Relations Unit,* (800) 865-7801 (answers questions regarding CASH, Medicaid, child care and food).

WASHINGTON STATE DEPARTMENT OF SOCIAL AND HEALTH SERVICES, HEALTH AND RECOVERY SERVICES ADMINISTRATION

Maximizes opportunities for patients with Medicaid to obtain appropriate, quality health services. PO Box 45505, Olympia, WA 98504-5505, (800) 562-3022, www.fortress.wa.gov/dshs/maa.

WASHINGTON STATE HUMAN RIGHTS COMMISSION
Provides information on filing discrimination complaints. (800) 233-3247, www.hum.
wa.gov.

WASHINGTON STATE INSURANCE COMMISSION, CONSUMER ADVOCACY AND OUTREACH DIVISION
Advises and advocates for consumers experiencing problems with group and individual
insurance policies related to contract compliance and state laws. Provides information
over the telephone. Does not have jurisdiction over self-insured plans, which are not
regulated under federal laws. PO Box 40256, Olympia, WA 98504-0256, (800) 562-
6900, www.insurance.wa.gov.

U.S. DEPARTMENT OF HEALTH AND HUMAN SERVICES, OFFICE FOR CIVIL RIGHTS
Provides information on filing discrimination complaints against companies receiving
federal funds. (877) 368-1019, www.hhs.gov/ocr/hippa.

U.S. DEPARTMENT OF LABOR, WAGE AND HOUR DIVISION
Can provide information about the Family and Medical Leave Act (FLMA), which
stipulates that companies with fifty or more employees must grant twelve weeks of
unpaid leave annually for certain family and medical situations. 111 3rd Avenue, Suite
755, Seattle, WA 98101-3212, (206) 553-4482.

Hospice and Palliative Care

GROWTH HOUSE
Provides in-depth information on end-of-life care. www.growthhouse.org.

HOSPICE FOUNDATION OF AMERICA
Gives general information on local hospice resource and contact information. www.
hospicefoundation.org.

NATIONAL FAMILY CAREGIVERS ASSOCIATION
Support and information for caregivers. (800) 896-3650, www.nfcacares.org.

NATIONAL HOSPICE AND PALLIATIVE CARE ORGANIZATION
Offers information and referrals for end-of-life care. (800) 658-8898, www.nhpco.org.

PARTNERSHIP FOR CARING: AMERICAN'S VOICES FOR THE DYING
Supplies end-of-life information and state-specific legal resources. (800) 989-9455,
www.partnershipforcaring.org.

Medical Research and Resources

AMC CANCER RESEARCH CENTER
Offers a toll-free telephone information line designed to help people diagnosed with cancer and their families, along with providing specific cancer-related resources. (800) 321-1557, www.amc.org.

AMERICAN MEDICAL ASSOCIATION
Abstracts from the *Journal of the American Medical Association* (JAMA) and nine specialty journals. www.ama-assn.org.

CANCER RESEARCH AND PREVENTION FOUNDATION
Prevention and early detection of cancer through scientific research and education. www.preventcancer.org.

CENTERWATCH CLINICAL TRIALS LISTING SERVICE
Listings of industry-sponsored and government-funded clinical trials that are actively recruiting. www.centerwatch.com.

FOOD AND DRUG ADMINISTRATION (FDA)
News from the FDA, including the latest and recently approved drugs for treating breast cancer. www.fda.gov.

MEDLINEPLUS HEALTH INFORMATION
Health information provided by the National Library of Medicine and the National Institutes of Health. www.medlineplus.org.

NATIONAL CANCER INSTITUTE (NCI), OFFICE OF CANCER SURVIVORSHIP
Studies the impact of cancer and its treatment to better understand the long-term needs of cancer survivors. http://cancercontrol.cancer.gov/ocs.

NATIONAL COMPREHENSIVE CANCER NETWORK
Learning center, clinical trials, clinical practice guidelines, treatment guidelines. www.nccn.org.

NATIONAL WOMEN'S HEALTH INFORMATION CENTER
A service of the Office on Women's Health (OWH) in the U.S. Department of Health and Human Services. www.4woman.gov.

NATIONAL INSTITUTES OF HEALTH (NIH), NATIONAL LIBRARY OF MEDICINE, CLINICAL TRIALS DATABASE
Regularly updated information about federally and privately supported clinical research. www.clinicaltrials.gov

RADIOLOGY INFO
Designed to answer questions related to the many radiologic procedures and therapies available. www.radiologyinfo.org.

Organizations and Resources for Specific Populations

Disabled

KING COUNTY METRO ACCESSIBLE SERVICES (ACCESS)
Provides low-cost and wheelchair-accessible transportation on a prescheduled basis, door-to-door. (206) 689-3113, www.kcmetrotransit.gov.

MEDICARE, CONSUMER SERVICES AND INFORMATION
Information about Medicare and the New Medicare Discount Drug Card. Also offers informational brochures on mammograms. (800) 633-4227, (206) 615-2354, www.medicare.gov.

WASHINGTON STATE DEPARTMENT OF LICENSING, DISABLED PERSON PARKING PRIVILEGES
Information and application forms for temporary disabled parking permits. A physician's certification of disability is required. (360) 902-3770, www.dol.wa.gov/vs/dpfaq.htm.

Foreign-Language Services

AMERICAN CANCER SOCIETY, REACH TO RECOVERY PROGRAM
Brochures available in various languages on breast cancer early detection, breast self-exam and diagnosis. (800) 227-2345, (800) 729-5588, (425) 741-8949 (Spanish-language translation and visitation services).

COMMUNITY HEALTH ACCESS PROGRAM (CHAP)
Assists callers with access to culturally and linguistically appropriate health care and social services for families and individuals regardless of their ability to pay. CHAP operates the information and referral line for the Washington Breast and Cervical Health Program (WBCHP) in King, Kitsap, Clallam and Jefferson counties (see WBCHP listing under "Low-Income," below). Se habla espanol and interpreters are available in various languages. (800) 756-5437, (206) 284-0331.

Y-ME
National organization for breast cancer information, support and counseling for breast cancer patients and families. 212 W Van Buren Street, Chicago, IL 60607, (800) 221-2141 (24-hour hotline, interpreters in 150 languages), (800) 986-9505 (Spanish), www.y-me.org.

Lesbian, Bisexual, Transgendered

MAUTNER PROJECT, THE NATIONAL LESBIAN HEALTH ORGANIZATION

The Mautner Project's mission is to improve the health of lesbians and their families through advocacy, education, research and direct services. On a national level, the organization provides phone support and assistance in locating local resources. 1707 L Street NW, Suite 230, Washington, DC 20036, (202) 332-5536 (voice/TTY), (202) 332-0662 (fax), mautner@mautnerproject.org, www.mautnerproject.org.

SISTAH TO SISTER

Community for lesbian, bisexual and transgendered women of color. For, by and about American Indian, African American, Latina, Asian, Asian Pacific Islander and Middle Eastern women. PO Box 5436, Tacoma, WA 98415, (253) 227-8533, sistahtosister@comcast.net, http://sistahtosister.home.comcast.net.

VERBENA

Committed to building and nurturing vibrant communities for lesbian, bisexual and queer women and transgendered individuals (LGBT) through health education, advocacy, support services and access to care. Lesbian Cancer Support Group meetings are held in the evenings the second and fourth Tuesdays of each month. An annual weekend retreat for LGBT cancer survivors is held at Harmony Hill (www.harmonyhill.org). Free mobile wellness screenings are available for LGBT women with limited resources; call the Positive Women's Network (888-651-8931). 511 E Pike Street, Seattle, WA 98122, (206) 323-6540, info@verbenahealth.org, www.verbenahealth.org.

Low-Income

CENTER FOR MULTICULTURAL HEALTH

Educational and outreach services. Participates in the Washington Breast and Cervical Health Program, which serves women aged 40 to 64 with low incomes and no health insurance (see listing below).105 14th Avenue, Suite 2C, Seattle, WA 98122, (206) 461-6900.

COMMUNITY HEALTH ACCESS PROGRAM (CHAP)

Assists callers with access to culturally and linguistically appropriate health care and social services for families and individuals regardless of their ability to pay. CHAP operates the information and referral line for the Washington Breast and Cervical Health Program in King, Kitsap, Clallam and Jefferson counties (see listing below). Se habla espanol and interpreters are available in various languages. (800) 756-5437, (206) 284-0331.

POSITIVE WOMEN'S NETWORK (PWN)

Connects uninsured and underinsured women in Island, King, San Juan, Skagit, Snohomish and Whatcom counties to free mammograms and yearly health exams. Also coordinates mobile health screenings to bring mammograms to culturally and geographically isolated women. For women who are living with life-challenging illness,

PWN has coping skills support groups, massage, Reiki treatments and wellness information. 3701 Broadway, Everett, WA 98012, (888) 651-8931 or (425) 259-9899, info@pwnetwork.org, www.pwnetwork.org.

WASHINGTON BREAST AND CERVICAL HEALTH PROGRAM (WBCHP)
Serves low-income, uninsured/underinsured women aged 40 to 64. Services include breast and cervical cancer screening exams, diagnostic services and prompt access to cancer treatment. Call the Community Health Access Program referral line for eligibility information and referral to participating clinics. (800) 756-5437, (206) 284-0331, www.doh.wa.gov/wbchp.

YWCA OF SEATTLE, WOMEN'S HEALTH OUTREACH (WHO)
Links medically underserved women to culturally appropriate women's health care providers for regular screening exams. Provides education on breast and cervical health and links uninsured and underinsured women aged 35 to 64 in King and Snohomish counties to free or low-cost mammograms, breast exams and pap tests. 2024 2nd Avenue, 2nd Floor, Seattle, WA 98121, (206) 436-8671, www.ywcaworks.org.

Military

MADIGAN ARMY MEDICAL CENTER AT FORT LEWIS
Offers multidisciplinary approach to services that include screening, diagnosis and treatment for active duty members, family members and retirees. Served by Reach to Recovery (a program of the American Cancer Society) and GANTS Breast Cancer Support Group. Also offers education, support services and treatment to members from Bremerton and Whidbey Island naval hospitals as well as McChord and Fairchild air force bases. Online access to the National Cancer Institute's Cancer Information Service. Breast Cancer Pathway (MCHJ-MHO), Tacoma, WA 98431, (253) 968-0975.

Women of Color/Ethnicity

AMERICAN INDIAN WOMEN'S WELLNESS PROGRAM
Offers free breast and cervical health screenings and follow-up services for low-income Native American women, aged 18 and over, in the service areas of the Chehalis, Nisqually, Shoalwater Bay, Skokomish and Squaxin Island tribes. South Puget Intertribal Planning Agency, 2970 SE Old Olympic Highway, Shelton, WA 98584, (360) 426-3990, witten@spipa.org, www.spipa.org.

CIERRA SISTERS INC.
An African American breast cancer survivor and support organization. Survivors and their supporters are invited to come to monthly meetings held in the evening the fourth Thursday of the month and in the afternoon the second Saturday of the month. PO Box 1634, Renton, WA 98057, (206) 505-9194, cierra_sisters@hotmail.com, www.cierrasisters.org.

INTERNATIONAL COMMUNITY HEALTH SERVICES (ICHS)
Provides tailored outreach, education, screening and referral services with interpretation/translation and access to breast cancer treatment through the Washington Breast and Cervical Health Program (see listing under "Low-Income," above), which serves women aged 40 to 64 with low incomes and no health insurance. Specifically serves Asian American women.
Holly Park Medical and Dental Clinic, 3815 South Othello Street, Seattle, WA 98118, (206) 461-4948;
International District Health Clinic, 720 8th Avenue South, Suite 100, Seattle, WA 98104, (206) 461-3235.

NATIONAL BLACK LEADERSHIP INITIATIVE ON CANCER
Works in conjunction with the Washington Breast and Cervical Health Program (see listing under "Low-Income," above). Outreach services and informational materials on breast cancer prevention and diagnosis. 105 14th Avenue, Suite 2C, Seattle, WA 98122, (206) 461-6900.

SEA MAR COMMUNITY HEALTH CENTER
A breast health outreach program offering educational services and family support groups to Hispanic women with breast cancer in Seattle/King County. Participates in the Washington Breast and Cervical Health Program, which serves low-income, uninsured/ underinsured women aged 40 to 64 (see listing under "Low-Income," above). 8720 14th Avenue S, Seattle, WA 98108, (206) 762-3730.

SEATTLE INDIAN HEALTH BOARD
Offers primary care on a sliding scale and referral services. Participates in the Washington Breast and Cervical Health Program, which serves low-income, uninsured/underinsured women aged 40 to 64 (see listing under "Low-Income," above). 611 Avenue S, Seattle, WA 98114, (206) 324-9360 or (206) 324-8484.

SHARSHERET
A national organization of cancer survivors dedicated to addressing the unique concerns of young Jewish women facing breast cancer. Connects young Jewish women recently diagnosed with breast cancer with volunteers. (866) 474-2774, www. sharsheret.org.

SISTAH TO SISTER
Community for lesbian, bisexual and transgendered women of color. For, by and about American Indian, African American, Latina, Asian, Asian Pacific Islander and Middle Eastern women. PO Box 5436, Tacoma, WA 98415, (253) 227-8533, sistahtosister@ comcast.net, http://sistahtosister.home.comcast.net.

SISTERS NETWORK
An African American breast cancer survivorship support group. National Headquarters, 8787 Woodway Drive, Suite 4206, Houston, TX 77063, (866) 781-1808, infonet@ sistersnetworkinc.org, www.sistersnetworkinc.org.

Seniors

MEALS ON WHEELS
Senior Services of Seattle/King County, Nutrition Project, Meals on Wheels, 2208 2nd Avenue, Seattle, WA 98101, (206) 448-5767, www.mowaa.org.

MEDICARE, CONSUMER SERVICES AND INFORMATION
Information about Medicare and the New Medicare Discount Drug Card. Also offers informational brochures on mammograms. (800) 633-4227, (206) 615-2354, www.medicare.gov.

SENIOR SERVICES
Advocates put seniors in touch with community resources. *Seattle*, (206) 448-3110; *Other locations*, (800) 972-9990, www.seniorservices.org.

Young Breast Cancer Patients

CANDLELIGHTERS INC.
For children with cancer and their parents. www.candlelighters.org.

FERTILE HOPE
Fertility information for young women faced with cancer treatment. www.fertilehope.org.

NORTHWEST YOUNG SURVIVORS
Dedicated to the concerns and issues unique to young women 40 and under with breast cancer. Supports and educates young women with breast cancer and educates young women about screening and prevention. (206) 683-4830, bcunder40@yahoo.com.

YOUNG SURVIVAL COALITION
National organization providing support for women age 40 and under. 155 6th Avenue, 10th Floor, New York, NY 10013, (212) 206-6610 or (877) YSC-1011, www.youngsurvival.org.

Hotlines

CANCER HOPE NETWORK
Confidential one-on-one support to people with cancer and their families. 877-HOPENET (467-3638), www.cancerhopenetwork.org.

CANCER LIFELINE
Twenty-four-hour emotional support and resource referral for Washington State. (800) 255-5505, (206) 297-2500 (in King County), www.cancerlifeline.org.

CANCERLINK
Confidential telephone support for patients, families and caregivers from trained volunteers who have had a similar experience. (877) 301-0005 (in Washington State), (425) 688-5266.

COMMUNITY RESOURCES ONLINE (CRISIS CLINIC)
Operates a 24-hour crisis line available to everyone in King County. (800) 244-5767, (866) 4-CRISIS or (206) 461-3222.

SUSAN G. KOMEN FOR THE CURE
Information on breast health or breast cancer concerns. *Breast Care Helpline*, (800) I'M AWARE (462-9273; 7am–3pm PST).

Y-ME
National organization for breast cancer information, support and counseling for breast cancer patients and families. 212 W Van Buren Street, Chicago, IL 60607, (800) 221-2141 (24-hour hotline, interpreters in 150 languages), (800) 986-9505 (Spanish), www.y-me.org.

Support Groups for Breast Cancer Patients

EASTERN WASHINGTON

PULLMAN REGIONAL MEDICAL CENTER
Breast Cancer Support Group
835 Bishop Boulevard
Pullman, WA 98163
(509) 336-7603
www.pullmanregional.org

WELLNESS HOUSE
Women's Cancer Support Group
210 S 11th Avenue, Suite 40
Yakima, WA 98902
(509) 575-6686

KITSAP AND OLYMPIC PENINSULAS

CANCER SUPPORT GROUP
Gig Harbor, WA
(253) 230-6244

CHRISTIAN CANCER CARE SUPPORT GROUP
Gig Harbor, WA
(253) 851-9216

HARRISON HOSPITAL
Breast Cancer Support Group
2520 Cherry Avenue
Bremerton, WA 98310
(360) 792-6885
www.harrisonhospital.org

JEFFERSON HEALTHCARE
Cancer Support Group
834 Sheridan Avenue
Port Townsend, WA 98368
(360) 385-2200, ext. 4648
www.jeffersonhealthcare.org

OPERATION UPLIFT CANCER SUPPORT
Group for Olympic Peninsula
PO Box 547
Port Angeles, WA 98362
(360) 457-5141

NORTH PUGET SOUND

ISLAND HOSPITAL
Breast Cancer Support Group
1211 24th Street
(360) 299-1342
Anacortes, WA 98221
www.islandhospital.org

PROVIDENCE EVERETT MEDICAL CENTER
Breast Cancer Support Group
Women Helping Women Group
916 Pacific Avenue
Everett, WA 98201
(425) 258-7255
www.providence.org/everett

SKAGIT VALLEY HOSPITAL
Breast Cancer Support Group
Cancer Care Center
1415 E Kincaid Street
Mount Vernon, WA 98273
(360) 428-8236
www.skagitvalleyhospital.org

WHIDBEY GENERAL HOSPITAL
Living with Cancer Support Group
101 N Main Street
Coupeville, WA 98239
(360) 678-7605 or (360) 321-6659
www.whidbeygen.org

SEATTLE AREA

CANCER LIFELINE
Breast Cancer Support Group
6522 Fremont Avenue N
Seattle, WA 98103
(800) 255-5505, (206) 297-2100
www.cancerlifeline.org

CIERRA SISTERS INC.
African American Breast Cancer Survivor and Support Organization
PO Box 1634
Renton, WA 98057
(206) 505-9194
cierra_sisters@hotmail.com
www.cierrasisters.org

EVERGREEN CANCER CENTER
Bosom Buddies
12303 NE 130th Lane
Kirkland, WA 98034
(425) 899-2265
www.evergreenhealthcare.org

GILDA'S CLUB SEATTLE
Breast Cancer Networking Group
1400 Broadway
Seattle, WA 98122
(206) 709-1400
www.gildasclubseattle.org

GROUP HEALTH CENTRAL
Women's Support Group
Main Building, D656
200 16th Avenue E
Seattle, WA 98112
(206) 326-3602
www.ghc.org

HIGHLINE MEDICAL CENTER
Breast Cancer Support Group
6251 Sylvester Road SW
Burien, WA 98166
(206) 431-5249
www.hchnet.org

NORTHWEST HOSPITAL
A Healing Place, Support Group for Advanced Breast Cancer
1560 N 115th Street
Seattle, WA 98133
(206) 920-5462

NORTHWEST HOSPITAL
Breast Cancer Support Group
Contact Cancer Lifeline
(800) 255-5505, (206) 297-2100
www.cancerlifeline.org

NORTHWEST YOUNG SURVIVORS
Breast Cancer Support Group
Seattle, WA
(206) 683-4830
bcunder40@yahoo.com

OVERLAKE HOSPITAL
Breast Cancer Support Group
Breast Reconstruction Group
1035 116th NE
Bellevue, WA 98004
(425) 688-5986
www.overlakehospital.org

THE POLYCLINIC
Breast Reconstruction Education Group
1145 Broadway
Seattle, WA 98122
(206) 860-2317

SEATTLE CANCER CARE ALLIANCE (SCCA)
Women Supporting Women with Cancer
825 Eastlake Avenue E (Sanctuary, 1st floor)
Seattle, WA 98109-1023
(206) 288-1082
www.seattlecca.org

SWEDISH CANCER INSTITUTE
Breast Cancer Education Support Group
1221 Madison
Seattle, WA 98104
(206) 386-6954 or (206) 386-2447
www.swedish.org

TEAM SURVIVOR NORTHWEST
Exercise Programs for All Women Affected by Cancer
200 NE Pacific, Suite 101
Seattle, WA 98195
(206) 732-8350
pm@teamsurvivornw.org
www.teamsurvivornw.org

VALLEY MEDICAL CENTER
Special Women
305 S 43rd Street
Renton, WA 98055
(425) 656-4002

VERBENA
Rainbow Women's Cancer Support Group
LGBT Community Center
511 E Pike Street
Seattle, WA 98122
(206) 323-6540

VIRGINIA MASON MEDICAL CENTER
Breast Reconstruction Support Group
925 Seneca
Seattle, WA 98111
(206) 223-6778 or (206) 223-6954, ext. 2
www.virginiamason.org

WOMEN'S HEALTH CENTER AT ST. FRANCIS
Breast Cancer Support Group
34503 9th Avenue S
Federal Way, WA 98003
(253) 944-4025

BREAST CANCER RESOURCE CENTER
Turning Point Support Group
3502 S 12th Street
Tacoma, WA 98405
(253) 752-4222
www.bcrcwa.org

LADIES IN PINK
Dinner meetings are on the first Tuesday of each month in a different area restaurant.
Call for location.
(253) 474-9396

MADIGAN ARMY MEDICAL CENTER AT FORT LEWIS
GANTS Breast Cancer Support Group
9040 Reis Street (Red Cross)
Tacoma, WA 98431
(360) 491-4590
Military ID required

MASON GENERAL HOSPITAL
Breast Cancer Support Group
901 Mt. View Drive
Shelton, WA 98584
(360) 426-5346
www.masongeneral.com

PROVIDENCE ST. PETERS HOSPITAL
A Touch of Strength Support Group
413 Lilly Road NE
Olympia, WA 98506
(360) 357-4088 or (360) 943-7032
www.providence.org/swsa

RAINIER ONCOLOGY AT THE GOOD SAMARITAN CANCER CENTER
Women's Cancer Support Group
400 15th Avenue SE
Puyallup, WA 98372
(253) 697-4863
www.goodsamhealth.org

SISTERS OF HOPE
Breast Cancer Support for Women of Color
Breast Cancer Resource Center
3502 S 12th Street
Tacoma, WA 98405

(253) 572-2683
sisterofhope@hotmail.com

ST. JOHN MEDICAL CENTER-PEACE HEALTH
I Understand Support Group
Women's Health Pavilion
1615 Delaware Street
Longview, WA 98632
(360) 501-3700
www.peacehealth.org/lowercolumbia

SWMC CANCER CENTER
Southwest Washington Medical Center
Breast Cancer Support and Education Group
400 NE Mother Joseph Place
Vancouver, WA 98644
(360) 514-2174
www.swmedicalcenter.org

Support for Family Members, Caregivers and Friends

CANCER LIFELINE
6522 Fremont Avenue N
Seattle, WA 98103
(800) 255-5505, (206) 297-2100
www.cancerlifeline.org

GILDA'S CLUB SEATTLE
1400 Broadway
Seattle, WA 98122
(206) 709-1400
www.gildasclubseattle.org

HARRISON HOSPITAL
Support One Another
2520 Cherry Avenue
Bremerton, WA 98310
(360) 792-6555
www.harrisonhospital.org

Support Groups and Organizations for Lymphedema

The following once-a-month groups are open to anyone with lymphedema who is interested in ongoing support and information. Call Cancer Lifeline at (206) 297-2100 for directions. For additional lymphedema support groups, call Cancer Lifeline or visit www.cancerlifeline.org.

BELLINGHAM

ST. LUKE'S HEALTH AND EDUCATION CENTER
3333 Squalicum Parkway
Third Tuesday of each month, 7:00-8:30 p.m.

EASTSIDE

CANCER LIFELINE–EASTSIDE
15355 SE 30th Place, Suite 240, Bellevue
First Wednesday of each month, 7:00-8:30 p.m.

EVERETT

SNOHOMISH PUD
2320 California Street
Second Thursday of each month, 7:00-8:30 p.m.

SEATTLE

DOROTHY S. O'BRIEN CENTER
6522 Fremont Avenue N (in the Green Lake neighborhood)
Third Monday of each month, 7:00-8:30 p.m.

SEQUIM

865 Carlsborg Road, Suite C
Third Tuesday of each month, 12:30-1:30 p.m.

TACOMA

BREAST CANCER RESOURCE CENTER
3502 S 12th Street
Second Thursday of each month, 6:30-8:00 p.m.

Lymphedema Organizations

BREAST CANCER PHYSICAL THERAPY CENTER
This organization specializes in women with breast cancer, helping them deal with range-of-motion problems and lymphedema. Publishes a booklet, *Recovery in Motion*, and has helped set up numerous breast rehabilitation centers throughout the United States. 1905 Spruce Street, Philadelphia, PA 19103, (215) 772-0160.

NATIONAL LYMPHEDEMA NETWORK
Nonprofit resource center that provides patients and professionals with information about prevention and treatment. Services include a hotline for referrals for medical treatment and physical therapy, general information and support in your area. Information packet available. Latham Square, 1611 Telegraph Avenue, Suite 1111, Oakland, CA 94616-2138, (800) 541-3259, www.lymphnet.org.

NORTHWEST LYMPHEDEMA CENTER
Local nonprofit that sponsors a support group, a newsletter and workshops. Offers self-care classes for patients. Dedicated to "providing education, information and resource referral to those interested in, or suffering from, lymphatic system disorders." 19625 62nd Avenue S, Building B, Suite 101, Kent, WA 98032, (206) 575-7775, www. nwlymphedemacenter.org.

Support Groups and Resources for Breast Cancer Genetics and Risk Evaluation

FORCE: FACING OUR RISK OF CANCER EMPOWERED
Support for women whose family history or genetic status puts them at high risk of getting ovarian and/or breast cancer, and for members of families in which this risk is present. www.facingourrisk.org.

HEREDITARY BREAST AND OVARIAN CANCER SUPPORT GROUP
Meets once every other month on a weeknight from 6:00 to 8:00 p.m. at the Team Survivor Northwest Office (200 NE Pacific Street, Suite 101, Seattle). For more information, contact the group facilitators, Ksenia Koon at (206) 288-6969 or kkoon@seattlecca.org.

HIGH RISK AND GENETICS SUPPORT GROUP
825 Eastlake Avenue E, Seattle, WA 98109-1023, (206) 667-7282, www.seattlecca.org

MADIGAN ARMY MEDICAL CENTER AT FORT LEWIS
Breast Cancer Initiative, Cancer Genetics Clinic, Tacoma, WA 98431, (253) 968-0786 or (253) 968-0756

SPOKANE GENETICS CLINIC
604 W 6th Avenue, Spokane, WA 99204, (509) 473-7115 or (800) 945-7115

SWEDISH MEDICAL CENTER
747 Broadway Avenue, Seattle, WA 98122-4037, (206) 386-2101

UNIVERSITY OF WASHINGTON MEDICAL GENETICS CLINIC
1959 NE Pacific Street, Seattle, WA 98195, (206) 598-4030

UNIVERSITY OF WASHINGTON/SEATTLE CANCER CARE ALLIANCE
BREAST AND OVARIAN CANCER PREVENTION CLINIC
825 Eastlake Avenue E, Seattle, WA 98109, (206) 288-6990

VRGINIA MASON MEDICAL CENTER
Hereditary Cancer Risk Assessment, Cathy Goetsch, (206) 223-6193

Transportation

ANGEL FLIGHT AMERICA
Provides access for patients in need seeking free transportation to specialized health
care facilities. (877) 621-7177, www.angelflightamerica.org.

KING COUNTY METRO ACCESSIBLE SERVICES (ACCESS)
Provides low-cost and wheelchair-accessible transportation on a prescheduled basis,
door-to-door. (206) 689-3113, www.kcmetrotransit.gov.

METRO REGIONAL REDUCED FARE PERMIT
A $3 permit for discount fares on transportation systems throughout the Puget Sound
region for people 65 or older or those disabled by cancer or cancer treatment. Requires
physician verification. (206) 553-3060, www.transit.metrokc.gov.

Wigs, Prostheses and Bras

Look in the Yellow Pages of your local telephone book under "wigs and
hairpieces" or do an Internet search. Many retailers provide catalogs and
pamphlets about their products and how to use them. Ask for copies. Some
retailers (e.g., Nordstrom) provide complimentary makeup applications
by professional makeup artists who have received training in the special
needs of cancer patients. Special makeup techniques and products are often
suggested.

Wigs, Prostheses and Bras—Local

BREMERTON

FARRELL'S HOME HEALTH
2326 Wheaton Way, Bremerton, WA 98310, (800) 233-6265, (360) 377-0164

CREATING CURVES
Kitsap County, (360) 265-3145 or (360) 307-8321

EDMONDS/EVERETT

KNUDSON HERB SURGICAL APPLIANCE AND HOSPITAL EQUIPMENT
2909 Hewitt Avenue, Everett, WA 98201, (425) 259-0144

OLYMPIA/CENTRALIA

NOVACARE/HANGER AND ORTHOTICS
Olympia, WA 98506, (360) 459-1099

SEATTLE AREA

GREATER SEATTLE PROSTHETIC AND ORTHOTIC CENTER
Numerous locations, see Yellow Pages.

MARY CATHERINE'S
901 Broadway, Seattle, WA 98122, (206) 322-1128

NORDSTROM
Numerous locations, see Yellow Pages or www.nordstrom.com.
Alderwood Mall, (425) 771-5755, ext. 1240
Bellevue Square, (425) 455-5800, ext. 1240
Downtown Seattle, (206) 628-2111, ext. 1240
Northgate, (206) 364-8800, ext. 1240
Southcenter, (206) 246-0400, ext. 1240
Tacoma Mall, (253) 475-3630, ext. 1240

NORTHWEST PROSTHETIC AND ORTHOTIC CLINIC
600 Broadway, Suite 190, Seattle, WA 98122, (206) 323-4040

SUN PRECAUTIONS
Provides head-to-toe sun protection clothing and some sunscreen products. 4015
Madison Street, Seattle, WA 98112, (800) 882-7860, (206) 322-7057, www.
sunprecautions.com.

JUDY'S INTIMATE APPAREL
4538 S Pine, Tacoma, WA 98407, (253) 474-5505

Wigs, Prostheses and Bras—National

AMERICAN CANCER SOCIETY (ACS)
Visit the website for a detailed listing of wig shops in your area. Click on "In your Community" and type in your zip code. Then under "Local Resources" select "Find More Local Resources." Also look under "Look Good . . . Feel Better." www.cancer.org.

BOSOM BUDDY
Prostheses. (800) 262-2789, www.bosombuddy.com.

CAMP HEALTHCARE
Prostheses, forms and bras. (800) 492-1088, www.camphealthcare.com.

COLOPLAST
Discreet self-supporting breast prostheses. Products are listed within the Medicare price range. Brochure and video available. (800) 726-6362, www.thebreastcaresite.com.

FREEMAN
Prostheses and bras. (800) 253-2091.

JC PENNEY
Prostheses and bras. Medicare may be billed under some circumstances. (800) 222-6161 (24-hour order line).

JODEE
Prostheses, bras and accessories. (800) 423-9038.

TLC CATALOG (TENDER LOVING CARE)
Products for hair loss, mastectomy products and cancer support products (wigs, hats, turbans, bras, prostheses). (800) 729-5588, www.tlccatalog.org.

Y-ME
Prostheses for a nominal mailing fee. (800) 221-2141.

"Racing for the Cure"

❦

Publications

Books

General

50 Essential Things to Do When the Doctor Says It's Cancer, revised ed., by G. Anderson (Plume, 1999).

After Breast Cancer: A Common-Sense Guide to Life After Treatment, by Hester Hill Schnipper (Bantam, 2003). Schnipper, a breast cancer survivor and an oncology social worker, helps prepare women for life after breast cancer by imparting information and advice in an intimate and direct manner. "Our lives have been changed in many ways," she writes, "and we have tried to be understanding and flexible about our possibilities . . . Our hearts and souls, however, need time to catch up."

Be a Survivor: Your Guide to Breast Cancer Treatment, 3rd ed., by Vladimir Lange, MD, (Lange Productions, 2005). Dr. Lange's physician wife was diagnosed with breast cancer. *Be a Survivor* was inspired by their desire to make the journey easier for others. Available in English and Spanish.

The Breast Cancer Book of Strength and Courage: Inspiring Stories to See You Through Your Journey, edited by Julie Fertig Panneton and Ernie Bodai, MD (Prima Lifestyles, 2002). Forty-seven short essays from breast cancer survivors.

A Breast Cancer Journey, 2nd ed. (American Cancer Society, 2004).

The Breast Cancer Survival Manual: A Step-By-Step Guide for the Woman with Newly Diagnosed Breast Cancer, 3rd ed., by John Link, MD (Owl Books, 2003). Written as a handbook for the newly diagnosed breast cancer patient so that she can get information and be empowered to participate in the decisions regarding her care and treatment. The resource section includes a list of organizations and a discussion of websites.

Breast Fitness: An Optimal Exercise and Health Plan for Reducing Your Risk of Breast Cancer, by Anne McTiernan, Julie Gralow and Lisa Talbott (St. Martin's Griffin, 2001). Guide to how exercise can reduce the risk for and recurrence of breast cancer, and how women can incorporate a safe and effective exercise program into their lives to fight against the disease.

Breast Implants: Everything You Need to Know, 3rd ed., by Nancy Bruning (Hunter House Publications, 2002). Comprehensive overview from the perspectives of consumer health advocates, the Federal Drug Administration and the medical community.

The Breast Reconstruction Guidebook: Issues and Answers from Research to Recovery, by Kathy Steligo (Carlo Press, 2003). There are many ways to reconstruct a breast. You can choose which option is right for you, but these choices require decisions and decisions require information. This book helps you understand the benefits and limitations to each reconstructive technique and what to expect each step of the way: before your surgery, in the hospital, during recovery and life beyond reconstruction.

Cancer Fitness: Exercise Programs for Patients and Survivors, by Anna Schwartz (Fireside, 2004). Increase your survival odds by creating and following an exercise program that counteracts the side effects of your treatment, speeds your recovery and reduces your risk of recurrence.

Cancer Lifeline Cookbook: Good Nutrition, Recipes and Resources to Optimize the Lives of People Living with Cancer, by Kimberly Mathai and Ginny Smith (Sasquatch, 2004). Empowering patients, caregivers and others to create healthful and nutritional meals.

A Cancer Survivor's Almanac: Charting Your Journey, by the National Coalition for Cancer Survivorship, edited by B. Hoffman, JD (John Wiley & Sons, Inc., 1996).

"Choice and Decision Making for Women with Breast Cancer," by S. Leigh, in *Contemporary Issues in Breast Cancer*, 2nd ed., edited by K. H. Dow (Jones and Bartlett, 2003).

Complementary Cancer Therapies, by D. Labriola (Prima Lifestyles, 2000).

Coping with Chemotherapy, updated ed., by Nancy Bruning (Avery, 2002). An excellent reference book, including the author's personal experience and commentary from health professionals.

Diagnosis Cancer: Your Guide through the First Few Months, expanded and updated ed., by W. S. Harpham (W. W. Norton, 2003).

Dr. Susan Love's Breast Book, 4th ed., by Susan Love, MD, with Karen Lindsey (Da Capo Lifelong Books, 2005). Written by a breast surgeon, this book contains information about breast diseases and breast health. A good resource for every woman, whether or not she has breast cancer. Also visit www.susanlovemd.org.

Earning a Living—Facing Forward, a Guide for Cancer Survivors (National Coalition for Cancer Survivorship, 1999).

Eating Well, Staying Well During and After Cancer (American Cancer Society, 2004). The experts at the American Cancer Society explore what you should eat and what you should avoid in order to stay strong and benefit from treatment.

Every Second Counts, by Lance Armstrong and Sally Jenkins (Broadway, 2003). Recounts Lance Armstrong's challenge of moving beyond his cancer experience, his first Tour de France victory and his celebrity status.

Fighting Cancer from Within, by M. Rossman (Owl Books, 2003). Focuses on visualization and imagery.

The First Look, by Amelia Davis, Nancy Snyderman, Loren Eskenazi and Saskia Thiadens (University of Illinois Press, 2000). Photographer Amelia Davis, whose mother had breast cancer, felt that women who had faced surgery and the loss of their breast(s) should be given a forum to express feelings about the experience and a means for others to see what they themselves saw upon their "first look" at a postmastectomy body.

It's Not About the Bike: My Journey Back to Life, reissued ed., by Lance Armstrong and Sally Jenkins (Berkley Trade, 2001). An inspirational true story about Lance Armstrong, a world-class athlete nearly struck down by cancer, only to recover and win the Tour de France, the multiday bicycle race famous for its grueling intensity.

Just Get Me Through This: The Practical Guide to Breast Cancer, by Deborah A. Cohen and Robert M. Geldfand, MD (Kensington, 2001). A survivor and an oncologist have produced a book that combines solid and well-summarized discussions on diagnostic, treatment and reconstruction options along with a plethora of tips on smaller but still difficult problems facing the breast cancer patient.

Journal: A Mother and Daughter's Recovery from Breast Cancer, by Annabel Clark, Lynn Redgrave and Barron Lerner (Umbrage, 2004). In 2002, British actress Lynn Redgrave learned she had breast cancer. Together with her daughter, Annabel Clark, then a photography student, she determined to record the experience through journal entries and Annabel's photographs. The result is a compelling document of treatment and recovery with an unprecedented level of intimacy. With heartrending honesty, in bittersweet moments as beautiful as they are difficult, the photographs and journal entries illustrate a personal journey through the leading cancer diagnosed in women today.

Living Through Breast Cancer, by Carolyn M. Kaelin and Francesca Coltrera (McGraw-Hill, 2005). The author is both a highly respected cancer surgeon who slipped through the looking glass on a journey that took her from doctor to patient. She is a breast cancer survivor who has had three lumpectomies, a mastectomy, chemotherapy and reconstructive surgery. Like an island of calm at the center of a storm of questions and anxiety, this book is a source of priceless information, understanding, support and guidance for women dealing with breast cancer.

Navigating Health Care, by the Washington State Insurance Commission (updated regularly). (800) 562-6900.

Reconstructing Aphrodite, by Terry Lorant and Loren Eskenazi (Syracuse University Press, 2001). Presenting the images and stories of women whose lives have been transformed after breast cancer, this volume offers a testament to the resilience of the human spirit triumphing in the face of adversity.

Relaxation and Stress Reduction Workbook, 5th ed., by Martha Davis, Elizabeth Robbins Eshelman and Matthew McKay (New Harbinger Publications, 2000). A comprehensive, easy-to-follow workbook that explores several techniques to reduce stress, including time management, meditation, assertiveness training, coping skills training, biofeedback, nutrition and exercise.

Spinning Straw into Gold, by Ronnie Kaye (Fireside, 1991). A counselor shares her personal breast cancer experience and recurrence with wit and understanding. Also included are suggestions for coping and full emotional recovery from breast cancer. An excellent resource for single women.

Uplift: Secrets from the Sisterhood of Breast Cancer Survivors, by Barbara Delinsky (Washington Square Press, 2001). The author, herself a breast cancer survivor, presents inspirational snippets from more than three hundred women sharing breast cancer tips and experiences. They recount the strategies that helped them through all aspects of cancer, including diagnosis, treatment, support groups and how to best conduct relationships with family and friends and in the workplace.

What Cancer Survivors Need to Know about Health Insurance, by K. J. Calder, MPS, and K. Pollitz, MPP (National Coalition for Cancer Survivorship, 2002). www.canceradvocacy.org.

Why I Wore Lipstick to My Mastectomy, by Geralyn Lucas (St. Martin's, 2004). The author was 27, happily working as a 20/20 producer, when she was diagnosed with breast cancer. This is an honest, perceptive memoir from a feisty survivor who is willing to discuss the daily details of her illness. The story of Lucas's recovery, and the birth of her daughter, make her book surprisingly optimistic and immensely empowering.

Support for Children

Our Family Has Cancer, Too!, revised ed., by Christine Clifford (University of Minnesota Press, 2002). Clifford shares her personal childhood experiences about her mother's breast cancer as well as her own experiences as a mother with breast cancer.

FOR AGES 8 AND YOUNGER

The Hope Tree: Kids Talk about Breast Cancer, by Laura Numeroff and Wendy S. Harpham, MD (Simon and Schuster, 2001).

Sammy's Mommy Has Cancer, by S. Kohlenberg and Lauri Crow (Brunner/Mazel, 2001).

FOR AGES 9 AND OLDER

When Someone in Your Family Has Cancer, by the National Cancer Institute. (800) 4-CANCER, www.cancer.gov/cancerinfo/your-family-has-cancer.

It Helps to Have Friends When Mom or Dad has Cancer, ACS Publication #4654 (American Cancer Society). (800) ACS-2345.

Breast Cancer: Questions and Answers for Young Women, by Carole G. Vogel (Twenty-First Century Books, 2001).

The Grieving Teen: A Guide for Teenagers and Their Families, by Helen Fitzgerald (Simon and Schuster, 2000).

Support for Significant Others

Breast Cancer Husband: How to Help Your Wife (and Yourself) During Diagnosis, Treatment and Beyond, by Marc Silver (Rodale, 2004).When Marc Silver became a breast cancer husband, he learned firsthand how frightened and helpless a husband can feel, and he searched in vain for a book that would give him the information and advice he so desperately sought. Now he has written a unique guide and useful resource packed with medical information, practical tips, psychological insight and coping strategies to help men help the women they love through this trying time.

Couples Confronting Cancer, Keeping Your Relationship Strong, by the American Cancer Society (American Cancer Society, 2003). Information about how others experience cancer, the problems it often causes and how to resolve, even prevent, those problems.

Helping Your Mate Face Breast Cancer: Tips For Becoming An Effective Support Partner, by Judy C. Kneece, RN, OCN (EduCare, 2001). Designed for mates of breast cancer patients to help them face the changes and challenges of meeting the vast support needs of the patient and themselves.

Terminal Illness

Healing Children's Grief: Surviving A Parent's Death from Cancer, by Grace H. Christ (Oxford University Press, January 2000).

The Needs of the Dying: A Guide For Bringing Hope, Comfort, and Love to Life's Final Chapter, by David Kessler (Harper, 2000).

Handbook for Mortals: Guidance for People Facing Serious Illness, by Joanne Lynn, MD, and Joan Harrold, MD (Oxford University Press, 2001).

Pamphlets

AMERICAN CANCER SOCIETY (ACS), (800) ACS-2345, WWW.CANCER.ORG:

After Diagnosis: A Guide for Patients and Families

Listen with Your Heart: Talking with the Person Who Has Cancer

For Women Facing Breast Cancer

Exercise after Breast Surgery

Understanding Radiation Therapy

Understanding Chemotherapy

Guide to Complementary and Alternative Medicine

Eating Well, Staying Well During and After Cancer

NATIONAL COMPREHENSIVE CANCER NETWORK (NCCN), (888) 909-NCCN, WWW.NCCN.ORG:

Breast Cancer Treatment Guidelines for Patients

Coping with Cancer. Bimonthly subscription magazine with articles on communication and coping with treatment and survivorship. Many doctors' offices and treatment facilities provide copies. Unfortunately, *Coping* is not indexed, making it difficult to identify and access articles. (615) 791-3859, copingmag@aol.com, www.copingmag.com.

CURE (Cancer, Updates, Research & Education). Quarterly magazine for cancer patients, survivors and caregivers, free to cancer patients. Website includes back issues, breaking news and web-exclusive articles. Available in many doctors' offices and treatment facility waiting rooms. Also produces a free monthly electronic mail update, CURExtra. (800) 210-CURE (2873), subs@curetoday.com, www.curetoday.com.

MAMM Magazine. A magazine about what women living with cancer experience. Women Cancer and the Community, 54 W 22nd Street, 4th Floor, New York, NY 10010, (646) 365-1350, www.mamm.com.

NATIONAL INSTITUTES OF HEALTH (NIH), WWW.NIH.GOV:

Taking Time (NIH Publication #04-2059). Support for people with cancer and the people who care about them.

Radiation Therapy and You: A Guide to Self-Help During Cancer Treatment (NIH Publication #03-2227).

Chemotherapy and You: A Guide to Self-Help During Cancer Treatment (NIH Publication #03-1136).

NATIONAL CANCER INSTITUTE (NCI), (800) 4-CANCER, HTTPS://CISSECURE.NCI.NIH.GOV/NCIPUBS:

Advanced Cancer: Living Each Day (NCI Publication #93-856).

Facing Forward Series: Life After Cancer Treatment (NCI Publication #P119 (2002). Designed to educate and empower cancer survivors as they face the challenges associated with life after cancer treatment. (800) 422-6237, www.qlmed.org/esperienza/guide/Life.html.

Patient Guide: Managing Cancer Pain (NCI Publication #P476).

Questions and Answers about Pain Control: A Guide for People with Cancer and Their Families (NCI Publication #P122).

Surgery Choices for Women with Early Stage Breast Cancer

When Cancer Recurs: Meeting the Challenge Again (NCI Publication #93-2709).

SUSAN G. KOMEN FOR THE CURE, (800) IM-AWARE, WWW. BREASTCANCERINFO.COM:

Chemotherapy

Facts for Life: Alternative and Complementary Therapy

Radiation Therapy

Glossary

adjuvant therapy: Medical treatment given in addition to the main treatment. The term usually refers to chemotherapy, endocrine therapy, radiation or immunotherapy administered before or after the main treatment to increase the chances of curing the disease or keeping it in check.

alopecia: Partial or complete hair loss that often occurs as a result of chemotherapy. In most cases, the hair grows back after treatment ends.

aneuploid: Cancer cells that contain either more or less DNA (chromosomes) than normal cells. About two-thirds of breast cancers are aneuploid.

anti-estrogens: Endocrine therapies, or drugs, that block or limit estrogen from reaching breast tissue and some breast cancers. Includes drugs that are selective estrogen-receptor modulators (SERMs), such as tamoxifen (Nolvadex), and selective estrogen-receptor downregulators (SERDs), such as fulvestrant (Faslodex).

aromatase inhibitors: Class of oral endocrine treatments, effective only in postmenopausal women, that work by lowering estrogen levels in the body. For example, anastrozole (Arimidex), letrozole (Femara) and exemestane (Aromasin).

atypia: See *hyperplasia.*

axillary lymph node dissection: Removes all the lymphatic tissue below the large vein in the armpit area (Level I and II nodes) and examines nodes for the presence of cancer. The number of nodes in this area varies from individual to individual.

benign: Not cancerous, nor malignant.

biopsy: The removal of a sample of tissue to see whether cancer cells are present. There are several kinds of biopsies. See *core biopsy, excisional biopsy, incisional biopsy, needle biopsy* and *stereotactic needle biopsy.*

biologic therapy (targeted therapy): Refers to a medication or drug that targets a specific pathway in the growth and development of a tumor. Such treatments often boost the body's immune system to fight against cancer.

bisphosphonates: Class of drugs most commonly used to prevent and treat osteoporosis, since their main action is to prevent bone breakdown. Used in addition to chemotherapy or endocrine therapy, bisphosphonates can reduce pain, fractures and other complications of bone metastases due to breast cancer.

blood count: A laboratory test to measure the number of red blood cells, white blood cells and platelets in a blood sample to determine the balance and number of these elements in the blood.

bone marrow: The soft tissue in the hollow of flat bones of the body that produces new blood cells.

breast reconstruction: Surgery that rebuilds the breast contour after mastectomy. A breast implant or the woman's own tissue is used. If desired, the nipple and areola may also be re-created. Reconstruction can be done at the time of mastectomy or at a later time.

breast self-exam (BSE): A method of checking one's own breasts for lumps or suspicious changes. BSE is an option for women beginning in their 20s. The goal with BSE is to identify any breast changes present and report them to a doctor or nurse right away.

calcification: Tiny calcium deposits within the breast, singly or in clusters, usually found by mammography. These are also called *microcalcifications.* They are a sign of change within the breast that may need to be followed by more mammograms or a biopsy. Calcifications may be caused by benign breast conditions or by breast cancer.

cancer: Not just one disease but rather a group of diseases. All forms of cancer cause cells in the body to change and grow out of control. Most types of cancer cells form a lump or mass called a *tumor.* The tumor can invade and destroy healthy tissue. Cells from the tumor can break away and travel to other parts of the body. This spreading process is called *metastasis.* When cancer spreads, it is still named after the part of the body where it started. For example, if breast cancer spreads to the lungs, it is still breast cancer, not lung cancer.

carcinogen: Any substance that causes cancer or helps cancer grow. For example, tobacco smoke contains many carcinogens that have been proven to dramatically increase the risk of lung cancer.

carcinoma: A malignant tumor that begins in the lining layer (epithelial cells) of organs. Approximately 80 to 90 percent of all cancers are carcinomas, and almost all breast cancers are carcinomas.

carcinoma in situ: An early stage cancer in which the tumor is confined to the organ where it first developed. The disease has not invaded other parts of the organ or spread to distant parts of the body. Most in situ carcinomas are highly curable.

chemoprevention: Therapies that use chemicals or drugs to reduce breast cancer incidence.

chemotherapy: Treatment with drugs to destroy cancer cells. Chemotherapy is often used in addition to surgery or radiation to treat cancer when it has spread, when it has come back (recurred) or when there is a strong chance that it could recur.

clinical trial: A research study that involves people and tries to answer specific questions. Each study is designed to test new methods of screening, prevention, diagnosis or treatment of cancer.

combination chemotherapy: Treatment using two or more anticancer drugs to achieve the most effective result.

control arm: The group of patients in a clinical trial that receives the standard or most commonly accepted treatment.

core biopsy: Similar to a needle biopsy, except the needle used is larger in order to remove more tissue from a suspicious area (such as a breast lump). See *needle biopsy.*

cyst: A fluid-filled mass that is usually benign. The fluid can be removed for analysis.

diagnosis: The process of identifying a disease by its signs or symptoms, and by using imaging procedures and laboratory findings. The earlier a diagnosis of cancer is made, the better the chance for long-term survival.

ductal carcinoma in situ (DCIS): Cancer cells that start in the milk passages (ducts) and have not penetrated the duct walls into the surrounding tissue. This is a highly curable form of early breast cancer. Also called *intraductal carcinoma.*

endocrine therapy (hormone therapy): Treatment with hormones, treatment with drugs that interfere with hormone production/action or the surgical removal of hormone-producing glands to destroy cancer cells or slow their growth.

estrogen: A female sex hormone produced primarily by the ovaries. In breast cancer, estrogen may promote the growth of cancer cells.

estrogen-receptor (ER) assay: A laboratory test done on a sample of the cancer tissue that determines if the breast cancer is stimulated by estrogen. Growth of normal breast cells and some breast cancers is stimulated by estrogen.

excisional biopsy: Surgical removal of an entire lump or suspicious tissue for diagnostic examination.

gene: A hereditary unit. A segment of DNA that contains information on hereditary characteristics, such as hair color, eye color and height, as well as susceptibility to certain diseases. Women who have BRCA1 or BRCA2 gene mutations (defects) have an inherited (genetic) tendency to develop breast cancer.

grade: The grade of a cancer reflects how abnormal it looks under the microscope. There are several grading systems for breast cancer, but all divide cancers into those with the greatest abnormality (Grade 3, or poorly differentiated), the least abnormality (Grade 1, or well differentiated) and those with intermediate features (Grade 2, or moderately differentiated). Grading is done by the pathologist who examines the biopsy specimen. Grading is important because higher grade (Grade 3) cancers tend to grow and spread more quickly and have a worse prognosis. A cancer's *nuclear grade* is based on features of the central part of its cells, the nucleus. The *histologic grade* is based on features of individual cells, as well as how the cells are arranged together.

HER-2: The HER-2/neu gene (human epidermal growth factor receptor-2) is responsible for making HER-2 protein, which is important for normal cell growth and development. About 25 percent of breast cancers have too much of (overexpress) this protein, causing cells to divide, multiply and grow more rapidly than normal.

hormone: A chemical substance released into the body by the endocrine glands, such as the thyroid, adrenals or ovaries. Hormones travel through the bloodstream and set in motion various body functions.

hospice: Palliative care involving families and caregivers for people in the final phase of illness. The care may take place in the patient's home or in a home-like facility.

hyperplasia: An abnormal increase in the number of cells in a specific area. By itself, hyperplasia is not cancerous, but when the cells are atypical (unlike normal cells) the risk of developing cancer is greater.

immune system: The complex system by which the body resists infection by microbes (such as bacteria or viruses). The immune system may also help the body fight some cancers.

immunotherapy: Treatments that promote or support the body's immune system response to a disease such as cancer.

incisional biopsy: Removal of a section of a suspicious lump through an incision. The section is then sent to a laboratory for analysis.

infiltrating cancer: See *invasive cancer.*

informed consent: A legal document that explains a course of treatment, for example, the risks, benefits and possible alternatives; the process by which patients agree to treatment.

in situ: Confined to the local area, preinvasive. See *carcinoma in situ.*

intraductal: Contained within the breast ducts.

intravenous (IV): A method of supplying fluids and medications using a needle inserted in a vein.

invasive cancer (infiltrating cancer): Cancer that has spread beyond the layer of cells where it started to nearby tissues. Some invasive cancers spread to distant areas of the body (metastasize), but others do not.

lat flap (latissimus dorsi flap): A method of breast reconstruction that uses the long flat muscle of the back by rotating it to the chest area to form a new breast mound.

linear accelerator: A machine used in radiation therapy to treat cancer.

lobular: Having to do with the lobules of the breast. See *lobules.*

lobular carcinoma in situ (LCIS): A very early type of breast cancer that develops within the milk-producing glands (lobules) of the breast and does not penetrate through the walls of the lobules.

lobules: The glands in a woman's breast that produce milk.

localized breast cancer: A cancer that started in the breast and is confined to the breast.

lumpectomy: Surgery to remove the breast tumor and a small amount of surrounding normal tissue.

lymphatic system: The tissues and organs (including lymph nodes, spleen, thymus and bone marrow) that produce and store lymphocytes (cells that fight infection) and the channels that carry lymph fluid. The entire lymphatic system is an important part of the body's immune system.

lymphedema: A complication in which excess fluid collects in the arms or legs. This may happen after the lymph nodes and vessels are removed in surgery, are injured by radiation or when a tumor interferes with normal drainage of the fluid.

lymph nodes: Small bean-shaped collections of immune system tissue such as lymphocytes, found along lymphatic vessels. They remove cell waste and fluids from lymph. They help fight infections and also have a role in fighting cancer.

lymphocytes: White blood cells that produce antibodies to destroy foreign organisms.

magnetic resonance imaging (MRI): A machine that creates images of the inside of the body. MRI uses a powerful magnet and radio waves to transmit images on a computer screen.

malignant tumor: A mass of cancer cells that may invade surrounding tissues or spread (metastasize) to distant areas of the body.

mammogram (mammography): An X-ray of the breast; a method of detecting breast cancer. A mammogram can show a developing breast tumor before it is large enough to be felt. Screening mammography is used to help find breast cancer early in women without any symptoms. Diagnostic mammography helps the doctor learn more about breast masses or the cause of other breast symptoms.

margins: The area of tissue that surrounds a tumor and is removed during surgery.

markers (tumor markers): Chemicals in the blood that are produced by certain cancers.

mastectomy: Surgery to remove all or part of the breast and sometimes other tissue. See *modified radical mastectomy* and *radical mastectomy.*

metastasis: The spread of cancer cells to distant areas of the body by way of the lymphatic system or bloodstream.

microcalcification: See *calcification.*

mitosis: The process of cell reproduction or division.

modified radical mastectomy: Surgery to remove the breast, skin, nipple, areola and most of the underarm lymph nodes on the same side, leaving the chest muscles intact. See *radical mastectomy.*

mortality rate: The rate at which people die as a result of a particular cause in a given population.

mucositis: Ulcerations or mouth sores caused by chemotherapy. See *stomatitis.*

mutation: The process in which a gene changes.

National Cancer Institute (NCI): A highly regarded federally funded research center in Bethesda, Maryland, and part of the National Institutes of Health (NIH), that conducts basic and clinical research on new cancer treatments and supervises clinical trials of new treatment throughout the United States.

needle biopsy: Removal of fluid, cells or tissue from a suspicious area (such as a breast lump) with a needle for examination under a microscope.

neoadjuvant therapy: Treatment given before breast surgery.

neoplasm: An abnormal growth (tumor). A neoplasm may be either benign or malignant. Cancer is a malignant neoplasm.

neutropenia: Low white blood count, one of the more serious side effects of chemotherapy.

nuclear grade: An estimation of the aggressiveness of the cancer made by judging the appearance of the cell's nucleus under the microscope. See *grade.*

oncogene: Genes that promote cell growth and multiplication. These genes are normally found in all cells. Oncogenes may undergo changes, causing cells to grow too quickly and form tumors.

oncologist: A doctor with special training in the diagnosis and treatment of cancer.

oncology: The study of cancer.

palliative treatment: Therapy that relieves symptoms, such as pain, but is not expected to cure the disease. Its main purpose is to improve the patient's quality of life.

palpation: Using the hands to examine. A palpable mass in the breast is one that can be felt.

pathologist: A doctor who specializes in the diagnosis and classification of diseases using laboratory tests, such as examination of tissue and cells under a microscope. The pathologist determines whether a tumor is benign or cancerous and, if cancerous, the exact cell type and grade.

placebo: An inert, inactive substance that may be used in studies (clinical trials) to compare the effects of a given treatment with no treatment.

platelet: A type of cell in the blood that helps it to clot.

poorly differentiated cells (undifferentiated cells): Abnormal cells that lack specialization in function and structure. Poorly differentiated cancers tend to grow and spread more quickly. See *grade.*

port (portacath): A device surgically implanted under the skin, usually in the chest, that enters a large blood vessel and is used to deliver drugs or fluids directly into the body.

primary site (tumor): The site where a cancer originally began. Primary cancer is usually named after the organ in which it starts.

progesterone: One of the female sex hormones released by the ovaries during every menstrual cycle to prepare the uterus for pregnancy and the breasts for milk production (lactation).

progesterone-receptor (PR) assay: A laboratory test done on a piece of the breast cancer that determines whether the cancer depends on progesterone for growth. Progesterone- and estrogen-receptor tests provide more complete information to help in deciding the best cancer treatment for the patient.

prognosis: A prediction of the course of disease; the outlook for the chances of survival.

prophylactic mastectomy: A mastectomy done before any evidence of cancer can be found, for the purpose of preventing cancer. This procedure is sometimes recommended for women at very high risk of breast cancer.

prosthesis: An artificial form, such as a breast prosthesis, that can be worn under the clothing after a mastectomy.

protocol: A formalized outline or plan, such as a description of what treatments a patient will receive and exactly when each should be given.

radiation oncologist: A doctor who specializes in using radiation to treat cancer.

radiation therapy: The treatment of cancer using high-energy rays (such as X-rays) to destroy cancer cells.

radical mastectomy (Halsted mastectomy): The removal of the entire breast, both pectoral muscles and all axillary lymph nodes on the same side.

radiologist: A doctor with special training in diagnosing diseases by interpreting X-rays and other types of diagnostic imaging studies, for example, computed tomography scans and MRI.

recurrence: Cancer that has come back after treatment.

red blood cells: Cells in the blood that carry oxygen to the tissues.

remission: Partial or complete disappearance of the signs and symptoms of cancer in response to treatment; the period during which a disease is under control. A remission may not be a cure.

second opinion: Recommendation from a doctor other than the initial physician.

sentinel lymph node biopsy: Test of the sentinel lymph node (the first lymph node or nodes in the chain of nodes that drains the area of the cancer). If this sentinel lymph node is free of cancer, the chance of cancer involvement farther up the lymph node chain is very low. In such a case, remaining lymph nodes are left intact, and a full axillary lymph node dissection is avoided.

side effect: A secondary effect from treatment.

silicone: Synthetic material used in breast implants because of its flexibility and durability.

S-phase fraction: The percentage of cancer cells that are replicating their DNA. DNA replication usually indicates that a cell is getting ready to split into two new cells. A low S-phase fraction is a sign that a tumor is slow-growing; a high S-phase fraction shows that the cells are dividing rapidly and the tumor is growing quickly.

staging: The process of finding out whether cancer has spread and, if so, how far. Staging of breast cancer is based on the size of the tumor, whether regional axillary lymph nodes are involved and whether distant spread (metastasis) has occurred. Knowing the stage at diagnosis is essential in selecting the best treatment and predicting a patient's outlook for survival.

stereotactic needle biopsy: A procedure that uses a needle guided into place by computer to obtain a biopsy specimen of a breast change seen on mammography.

stomatitis: Inflammation or ulcers of the mouth area. This condition can be a side effect of some chemotherapies. See *mucositis.*

tamoxifen (Nolvadex): A drug that blocks the effects of estrogen on many organs, such as the breast. See *anti-estrogens.*

T-cell: White blood cells that are a part of the body's immune system.

terminal: Ending in death; fatal.

tissue expander: A breast implant that is placed under the chest muscle. The chamber is slowly expanded with injections of salt water. Expanders are used in breast reconstruction to slowly stretch the chest muscle.

TNM classification: A system to classify cancers by the size of the tumor (T), lymph node involvement (N) and distant metastasis (M; whether it has spread to other sites in the body).

TRAM flap (transverse rectus abdominus myocutaneous flap): A method of breast reconstruction that moves abdominal muscle, skin and fat under the skin to the chest to form a new breast mound.

tumor: An abnormal lump or mass of tissue. Tumors can be benign (not cancerous) or malignant (cancerous).

tumor marker: See *markers.*

undifferentiated cells: See *poorly differentiated cells.*

well-differentiated cells: Cancer cells that look similar to normal cells from the same organ. Usually a less-serious cancer. See *grade.*

NOTE: Glossary words appear in *italics* throughout this guide's text.

Index

NOTE: Terms that are defined in the Glossary appear below in *italics*.

anticancer, 12–13
for insomnia, 114
ductal carcinoma in situ (DCIS), 4, 27, 29, 33

Eastern Cooperative Oncology Group (ECOG), 70
electrical impedance imaging, 18
emotions surrounding breast cancer, 102–104
managing, 115
research on, 136
endocrine therapy, 28, 30, 44, 46–48, 52, 96
bisphosphonates and, 52, 135
oral, 46
research, 130
endometrial cancer, 10, 12, 47, 130
epoetin alfa (Procrit, Epo), 50
epothilones, 133
estrogen
levels as related to cancer, 46, 48
replacement therapy, 112
research on, 131
and risk, 8, 12
supplemental, 9, 112
tests for, 28
vaginal, 9, 116
exemestane (Aromasin), 13, 28, 46
exercise
in CAM therapies, 76, 79
for menopausal side effects, 112
during physical rehabilitation, 86–87
as protective factor, 12, 14, 82, 117, 137
and relaxation, 115
external beam radiation, 40, 41

Family and Medical Leave Act (FMLA), 123
family history, as risk factor, 10, 131
family issues surrounding cancer, 104–106
farnesyl transferase inhibitors, 135
fatigue, 56, 86, 87, 93, 106, 136. *See also* side effects
fear / anxiety, 102, 104, 107, 114
fenretinide, 130
Fertile Hope, 65
fertility issues, 65
fibroadenomas, 9
filgrastim (Neupogen), 50, 57
fine needle aspirate (FNA), 17
5-fluro-uracil (5-FU), 49
fluorescence in situ hybridization (FISH) testing, 51
fluoxetine (Prozac), 113
follow-up care, 92

Food and Drug Administration (FDA), approvals, 18, 47, 72, 117, 128
Fred Hutchinson Cancer Research Center, 9
friends. *See* support groups
Fulvestrant (faslodex), 47–48

gabapentine (Neurontin), 113
gemcitabine (Gemzar), 49
genes
analysis, 131
cancer-related, 28, 128, 129
susceptibility (BRCA1 and BRCA2), 10
genetic(s)
research, 129
as risk factor, 8
testing, 11
genomic profiling, 131
Gilda's Club, 79
grief surrounding cancer, 102–103
gynecologic exams, 92

hair loss, 105, 106. *See also* alopecia
health care wishes (durable power of attorney, directives, wills), 124–125
Health Insurance Portability and Accountability Act (HIPAA), 122
heart attack risk, 47
heart disease, 82, 117, 118
heat therapy (moxibustion), 79
Herceptin, 51, 134
hereditary. *See* genetic(s)
HER-2, 28, 51, 128, 134
herbal medicines / herbs, 77, 78, 79
homeopathy, 77
hormone-receptors, 45, 131
tests, 28
hormone replacement therapy (HRT), 9
hormones
postmenopausal, 9
role of, 8
hormone therapy, 128. *See also* endocrine therapy
hospice care / services, 98–99
hot flashes and night sweats, 112–113, 136
human genome, 128
hydrotherapy, 78
hyperplasia, 9, 33
hysterectomy, 9

ibandronate (Bondronat, Boniva), 52, 117
IBIS II Trial, 13, 130
IGFR, 136
imaging techniques, 18, 29

tipifarnib (Zarnestra), 135
tissue density, as risk factor, 9
tissue transplants, 35–36
toremifene (Fareston), 47
toxicity. *See* side effects
traditional Chinese medicine (TCM), 77, 79
TRAM flap, 37, 132
trastuzumab (Herceptin), 51, 128, 134
treatment, cancer, 137
    incorporating CAM, 76–80
    conventional, 76
    decisions, 23
    evaluation of, 68
    metastatic (Stage IV), 45–46
    options, 29–30, 44
    post-, 109
    at recurrence, 96
    of young women with breast cancer, 65
triazolam (Halcion), 114
tumor
    grade, 28
    markers, 28–29, 92
    size, 26, 45, 131
tumor suppressor genes, 28, 129
Tykerb, 134

ultrasound, 17, 18, 29
U.S. Department of Labor, Wage and Hour Division, 123
U.S. Food and Drug Administration (FDA), 35
uterine cancer, 8, 130. *See also* endometrial cancer

vaccines, cancer, 136
vaginal dryness and lubricants, 116, 136
vascular endothelian growth factor (VEGF), 51

vinorelbine (Navelbine), 49
volunteer activities, 140–141

Washington State
    Basic Health Plan, 120
    Department of Health (licensure), 78, 79, 80
    Department of Social and Health Services, 123
    health insurance, 121
    Insurance Commissioner's office, 121, 123
    mandatory breast cancer-related health benefits, 122
    Medical Assistance Administration, 120
    public assistance, 120
    SHIBA, 121, 122
Western Washington Breast Cancer Treatment Centers, 144 (Appendix A)
white blood cells (*T-cells*), 57. *See also* neutrophils
Women's Health Initiative (WHI) trial, 9
Women's Intervention Nutrition Study (WINS), 137
written record, 21

X-ray, and radiation therapy, 40

Y-ME, 61, 121
yoga, 86, 113, 115

Zofran, 58
zoledronic acid (Zometa), 52, 135
zolpidem (Ambien), 114
Zometa, 135